HOW TO BE A BADASS LAWYER

The Unexpected & Simple
Guide To Less Stress and Greater
Personal Development Through
Mindfulness and Compassion

BY
CLAIRE E. PARSONS

ISBN: 979-8-9870886-1-6 (hardback)
ISBN: 979-8-9870886-0-9 (paperback)
ISBN: 979-8-9870886-2-3 (ebook)

TESTIMONIALS

"Claire's devotion to mindfulness and compassion is something the legal industry has needed for decades. Better still, she presents her material in a practical and accessible manner that enables any lawyer to apply these principles to their lives."
— Jeremy W. Richter, attorney and author of
Level Up Your Law Practice

"It's normal for attorneys to be skeptical, but vetted studies show the benefits of meditation. At a certain point, the success of a law practice means thinking about what is best for you as a lawyer long-term. Mindfulness meditation is one way that lawyers can focus on what's most important to them."
— Kristin Tyler, Partner, Garman Turner Gordon LLP, Las Vegas, Nevada, and Co-Founder of LAWCLERK Legal

"We all go through challenging times, and having the capacity to navigate them with compassion is at the heart of resilience. I'm thrilled that Claire has written this book for the legal profession. I can't imagine a better guide."
— Laura Banks, Certified Compassion
Cultivation Training© Instructor

"Claire is a thought leader in the legal profession, and she's sharing her knowledge of mindfulness and compassion at a time when lawyers and law firms need it."
— John Trimble, Partner,
Lewis Wagner, LLP Indianapolis

"Anyone who knows mindfulness knows it can be hard. Claire breaks it down in a practical way and shares how compassion can make a huge difference for lawyers whether they meditate regularly or not."

— Talar Herculian Coursey, General Counsel of Vista Lincoln Ford of Southern California, active yogi, and author of *Ralphy's Rules for Living the Good Life* and co-author of *#Networked* and *Women in Law*

"Claire is a great person to speak to lawyers about mindfulness, compassion, and wellness because she lives the life of a lawyer and knows how to speak their language."

— Tom MacIntosh, experienced law firm IT Administrator and Mindful Leadership Coach, certified at Reiki Level III as a meditation teacher and in emotional intelligence

"I've had the pleasure and privilege to get to know Claire, first online through LinkedIn, then through her content and videos online, and finally through various presentations she's given. Her presence, her perspective, and her advice bring peace. Her whole being brings peace. If you want to learn to be centered, to be in the moment, to find your Zen, follow Claire, listen to what she has to say, and read this book."

— Frank Ramos, Partner, Clarke Silvergate, Miami, Florida

"Claire's knowledge and practical understanding of what litigators face puts her in the ideal position to help lawyers navigate their practice with compassion for others and compassion for themselves, which is why I asked Claire to speak to our firm about compassion practices. Contrary to the popular image, it is compassion and not the absence of compassion that makes a truly badass lawyer. Claire shows us the way to becoming better lawyers, and people, through compassion practices and meditation. I am grateful that she is sharing her experience and wisdom about these transformational practices."

— Eddie Medina, Partner,
Foley & Mansfield, Miami, Florida

"Claire is a natural storyteller. She doesn't just teach compassion and mindfulness, rather she helps you feel it and experience it for yourself so that you can put it to use in your life."

— Christon Halkiotis, CEO & Managing Attorney
at the Law Office of Christon S. Halkiotis, PLLC,
Greensboro, North Carolina

"Meditation changed my life. The benefits took some time to emerge but with patience and practice I found myself becoming less reactive to the challenges of life. I consider the time and money I invested to learn meditation as well worth it because they were investments in myself."

— Tahmina Watson, Immigration Attorney and
author of *Legal Heroes* and *The Startup Visa*.

DEDICATION

This book is for all the lawyers who want to find a better way to practice law, who want to find a little peace for themselves even as they face the hard parts of life, and who want to learn to trust themselves more and for the countless lives they can change for the better if they do.

FOREWORD

If life or law practice has sent you unforeseen challenges, you are in good company, and we welcome you into the fold. Read on for inspiration, information, and practical skills about how mindfulness and compassion can help you transform those challenges into a journey that just might change your life and the world for the better.

Neither Claire Parsons nor I could have guessed what paths we would take after law school. We thought we'd be lawyers who just happened to have families. As it turns out, life and law practice forced us both to be more than that. It forced us to reach deeper into our strengths than we ever knew we would have to so that we could show the world the badass lawyers we are and help others own their strengths as well.

Despite being law school classmates, the force that ended up bringing us together was a surprising one: motherhood. In particular, Claire and I both shared the challenge of struggling with motherhood as lawyers. I struggled to navigate my way through law school and then practice in big law with two small children. Claire struggled with her mental health after having her first daughter. My struggle caused me to found MothersEsquire to advocate for lawyer moms. Claire's caused her to develop a passion—and truly to find her inspiring voice—in order to advocate for lawyers' minds and their inherent well-being.

Claire's mission in this book is simple: to help lawyers, firms, and companies see that the work of care, including self-care, is powerful and essential to happiness as a lawyer and the long-term success of the profession. Knowing how to cultivate mindfulness and compassion is critical because any practicing lawyer knows that all the life hacks and self-help books in the world can't change the fact that law practice is stressful. Coaches, therapists, and doctors might tell you to manage or reduce stress, but how do you do that in a profession that deals in conflict and risk assessment and requires continually helping clients navigate through adversity?

The truth is there is no magic way to make law practice less stressful, though needed systemic and cultural changes can help. While we continue to advocate for those larger systemic changes in the profession, it is important to know what lawyers practicing law right now can do to care for themselves while that change unfolds (which hopefully will allow them to be a part of the changes). Attorneys can learn to respond to stress in a new way. This includes learning to recognize the signs of stress, limiting how much their minds create unnecessary stress, and honoring and caring for their emotions. This is what mindfulness and compassion can help you do.

What's more, Claire teaches these tools without asking any lawyer or firm to fix or change themselves. To make any necessary change, individuals and organizations may have to change practices and policies, and they may have to learn new ways of doing things. It stands to reason that one cannot expect different results from maintaining the same course of conduct. The truth remains, though, that nobody wants to be told that their way of being is "deficient" or that they are not already enough. That message, unfortunately, is far too prevalent today for lawyers who are already doing so much.

Claire knows this "fix yourself" messaging because she has lived through it. She has experienced life as an associate with a baby who wouldn't sleep through the night while Claire tried to prepare for an impending trial. She experienced life as a law firm partner trying to support both her family and staff through challenging times while maintaining her productivity. She has experienced the demands of client needs, family obligations, and community work.

The practical guidance found in this book is built on Claire's lived experiences, as well as years of training and mindfulness practice. Compassion and mindfulness have helped Claire manage the demands of her career and life and to thrive while doing so. Through my friendship with Claire over the years, I have witnessed Claire use her passion for this practice to guide others, and like the readers of her words will experience, I have personally benefited from Claire's firm and gentle guidance on using compassion and mindfulness in my life.

What you will discover by reading more is that Claire teaches mindfulness and compassion in a way that lawyers can read, understand, and use. One of the things that stood out to me early on with Claire is that she loves to joke and tell stories. Though she's analytical and deeply thoughtful by nature, she puts her sense of humor and storytelling to work in all her writing.

It's not uncommon for her to blend ancient philosophy, a reference to *Parks and Recreation* or *Star Wars,* and a story from her life to elucidate truths about the human condition. This makes her works not only meaningful but also engaging and enjoyable to read. Since Claire is writing to help other lawyers build happy and healthy lives in the law, it makes sense that she would write about that in a fun, joyful, and even playful way.

I have worked to build a community and a platform for moms in the legal profession because I believe it will be infinitely better off with more caregivers in it. Claire believes that the legal profession will be better off if more of us knew how powerful care can be, how to reconnect with our innate ability to care, and how to unlock it to care for ourselves, our clients, and our communities.

Having seen Claire share these strategies for the bar over the last several years, I am thrilled that she has shared this practical, accessible resource to help lawyers learn these essential skills in a totally new and refreshing way.

Michelle Browning Coughlin, Esq., practicing intellectual property attorney, mom, Founder of MothersEsquire, Member of ABA Commission on Women, author of *My Mom the Lawyer*

GREETINGS FROM YOUR MINDFUL LOCAL COUNSEL

Hello, dear reader. Yes, you are in the right place. If you feel nervous or skeptical, don't worry. You are doing the right thing by reading this book. Lawyers like us don't always feel comfortable going into new territory. I know this may be new for you.

What do you normally do when you find yourself handling a case in a new jurisdiction or outside of your normal practice area? You got it. You find local counsel or call an attorney friend who knows the law in that area better than you do. Maybe you didn't think of it this way when you bought the book, but you are doing the same thing here.

Consider me your local counsel of mindfulness and compassion. I'm another lawyer who has gone through this before. I'm here to answer your questions and calm your fears about how all this mindfulness stuff goes. Like any good local counsel, I can share what the customs are, interpret some concepts and lingo, and help you find the best approach.

I know this not just because I'm certified to teach mindfulness and compassion and have done so for thousands of lawyers across the country but also because I've incorporated those skills into my life and law practice for the past ten years.

By opening this book, though, you have not merely made the wise decision to ask for help but also acknowledged something really important. You have shown that you believe a better way of practicing law and living life is possible. I know law practice doesn't make this easy for us, and I'm used to billable hours, so I know your time is limited and valuable.

That better way you were looking for when you discovered this book is out there. You can stop worrying so much about making mistakes and missing deadlines. You can stop constantly thinking about work when you are with the people you love. You can stop reacting with judgment and resisting life all of the time. You can learn to relax and manage your stress. You can be a kind person and a badass lawyer.

And the good news? It doesn't require you to change who you are or to stop being a strong counselor and competitor. All that is required is a willingness to see who you are and to look at life in a new way. I have done this myself, and I know it can feel daunting at first. I'll be here with you step by step, I'll make it as simple as I can, and we'll move very gradually.

You deserve to see exactly how much of a badass lawyer you can be, and the world needs to see it too. Keep your mind open, turn the page, and let's go.

- Your Mindful Local Counsel and Soon-to-Be Author/
Lawyer/Meditation Teacher Friend,

Claire E. Parsons

TABLE OF CONTENTS

PART III:
REAPING THE BENEFITS OF
MINDFULNESS AND COMPASSION

INTRODUCTION (WHY I WROTE THIS BOOK AND WHY YOU WANT TO READ IT)

I remember when I first started exploring mindfulness ten years ago. I had doubts, was skeptical, etc. As a lawyer, why wouldn't I be? I had read about the concepts for years but didn't start meditating until one of the busiest times in my life. I had a one-year-old daughter who still didn't sleep through the night. I was preparing for a huge trial. My caseload was so out of control that I cried in my office one day from sheer overwhelm when I saw I had overlooked a deadline and had to work through the night to draft a motion due the next morning.

Have you ever experienced this (or something similar)? Then you're not alone.

Overwhelm drove my anxiety and rumination to unbearable levels so that I couldn't rest even when I had the time to do so. When I first sat to meditate, it was more of a surrender than the start of a quest for personal growth. I didn't know if the practice would help me improve my life. I tried stopping for a moment because I didn't know what else to do, and research said it could help.

To my complete astonishment, it did. Physical signs of stress immediately reduced. My overthinking gradually disappeared. Over time, I even confronted my tendencies to rush, resist, and judge myself and others and developed the ability to relax, slow down, and greet life with kindness and a sense of humor. As you can imagine, this changed almost everything for me!

Meditation helped me thrive in a practice that I wasn't sure I could manage as an associate. It helped me learn to love and trust myself despite years of self-criticism and doubt. It helped me not take every problem in my family personally so I could be in a better position to enjoy my loved ones in the good times and support them in the bad ones. In short, meditation transformed my life and law practice from a depressed, anxious, and conflict-ridden one into a happy, confident, and vibrant one.

I'd like to say, looking back, that there were lots of resources available to help me learn. I am thankful for many fine meditation teachers who shared their teachings. In reality, though, I was inspired to start teaching mindfulness and compassion to other lawyers and professionals because there wasn't much out there that spoke directly to me as a practicing lawyer.

Why does this matter? It matters because mindfulness and compassion are not mere concepts. To have an impact, they need to be lived experiences.

Most books written for lawyers about mindfulness or wellness available when I started meditating did not speak to my lived experience. Some were bogged down in lingo or abstract philosophy that diluted their practicality. It was also hard to miss the trend that so many of those books were written by people who had never practiced law or had stopped practicing. These works, therefore, explained mindfulness but didn't tell me how to use it. Though they identified practices to try, they didn't help me envision how they would fit into my life as a practicing lawyer at a midsize firm in the Midwest.

This was a blessing in disguise for me, and it is now a gift I can share with you. Because I didn't have a clear guide that told me what meditation styles worked best for lawyers, I took what I could from the resources available and built my own meditation practice. I mixed and experimented and tinkered over the years to find a practice that worked for me.

What did I learn? I learned that mindfulness was, as judges sometimes say, "necessary but not sufficient."

Breath practice was a great start, but it got stale after a while. When I added practices to learn compassion and body awareness, meditation became more vibrant, real, and useful in my everyday life.

After I started teaching and writing about meditation years ago, I was surprised to learn that most lawyers didn't know about either concept. They knew that mindfulness could help them, and many had tried meditation before, following the standard practice of focusing on their breath. They also told me, of course, that meditation had not worked for them because they couldn't clear their mind, sit still, or stick with a practice.

Sure, meditation can be hard, but lawyers are used to hard things. What gives?

From talking to and teaching lawyers across the nation about mindfulness, compassion (the ability to be present with and accepting of difficulty) is the missing ingredient. I was afraid to start teaching the practice at first, but I couldn't resist because it had helped me so much. When I saw how lawyers, even seasoned litigators from huge law firms, reacted when they tried loving-kindness practice, I knew it wasn't just me.

Lawyers tend to be a tough bunch of people, but sometimes toughness can become brittle. In our stressful jobs, it helps to add suppleness into our lives to balance the struggle we experience in law practice every day. This is what compassion offers to us lawyers: a new way of relating to stress and struggle.

This is a game changer because lawyers can't make our jobs stress-free, but we can change how we respond to stress.

Loving-kindness offers a new way of responding to stress because it helps you remember what kindness is, what it feels like, and how to offer it to yourself and others at critical times. When I did this practice, I found that I could treat myself kindly when I struggled in meditation. Soon after, I noticed that I automatically treated myself and others with kindness when life was hard.

As a litigator, mom to young girls, and law firm partner, my life is frequently hard. Meditation, however, which includes practice in mindfulness and compassion, keeps my skills of presence and kindness sharp so they are always available when I need them. While I have used therapy, medication, and coaches to address mental health challenges or manage stress, it is empowering and, frankly, convenient to be able to handle more situations on my own. Those are the very skills you will discover in this book.

You will not merely learn mindfulness here, though you will explore ways to get clarity about your thoughts and breathing strategies to calm down. Instead, with this book, you will try practices to help you understand your whole being—mind, body, and heart. More significantly, you will learn and try those practices step-by-step, and with the support of a fellow practicing lawyer, so you don't have to make your own recipe for practice from scratch like I did.

Just like any good lawyer would, I will break this process into elements. This will help you build discrete skills as you cultivate a greater understanding of mindfulness and compassion as a whole.

As in any brief, you'll get the background facts and learn concepts so that you can understand what compassion is and how it interacts with mindfulness to create overall well-being. Then, you will explore practices that can help you build mindfulness, including awareness of your thoughts and body and emotional intelligence. With that foundation, you will learn the transformational practice of loving-kindness.

I created this book as a guide that you can use to develop your own meditation practice over the course of four weeks. Though that may seem ambitious if you have not meditated before, I urge gradual growth and self-kindness throughout. Over the course of these weeks, you will build skills one at a time while increasing your tolerance for meditation gradually from less than five to twenty minutes (0.1 to 0.4 hours). You will also build skills for noting thoughts, reducing judgment and resistance, creating body awareness, and understanding your emotions.

This is critical because those are all the skills you need to respond better to stress, not by avoiding it but by greeting it with compassion.

Research tells us that mindfulness and compassion practices can increase happiness, improve work performance and relationships, reduce rumination, and minimize stress. To obtain these benefits, it is essential to do the practices and experience mindfulness and compassion for yourself.

In terms of reading this book, my recommendation is to read Chapters 1 to 3. If you have a physical or mental health condition that causes you concern based on what you read, take the time to consult with a doctor or mental health provider for their guidance and support. Then, proceed with Chapters 4 to 7 and strive to do the practices daily as designated each week. I do not suggest daily practice to force you to strive for perfection. If you miss a day, just try the next one. A daily practice, however, will increase the chances that you make meditation a lasting habit.

Chapters 8 to 10 are there to help you assess your practice, reflect on how the practices have affected you, and envision the possibilities that might await your life with further practice. As you read or any time thereafter, I invite you to follow me on LinkedIn or subscribe to my blog, Brilliant Legal Mind (www.brilliantlegalmind.com).

If you are unsure or have questions about the practices, the blog may have articles, meditations, and resources that can help, and I invite you to email or message me if not. Though technology has empowered us to learn meditation on our own, it is a practice best done in community. Don't be a stranger as you go about this process.

I know what it is like to start exploring things like meditation that you never thought you'd want or need. I know it is hard to feel like you need extra help and strategies for self-care when other lawyers all seem to be happily busy and have no problems. The strategies in this book, though, aren't extra, and they aren't weird. They go directly to the heart of your human experience and your work as a lawyer.

You aren't weak or strange or flawed for reading this book to find a better way. You are smart, brave, practical, and kind.

Mindfulness and compassion totally changed my life and started me on a path of personal development I could never have imagined without them. Because of that experience, I have served my clients through times of trouble, my profession, and my community as a leader and teacher, and I have been there for my family when they needed me most. Meditation helped me learn how to love and care for myself, and that is what allowed me to help so many others.

I wrote this book because I know there are other lawyers out there looking for a better way. I found a better way just by taking the first step. With this book, I hope you feel a little less alone and more sure as you take yours. Take a breath and turn the page so you can learn what a badass lawyer you are.

ABOUT THE AUTHOR
(THE TRUTH BEHIND
MY LINKEDIN PROFILE)

Hello. I am Claire E. Parsons, a local government, litigation, and employment lawyer at Wood + Lamping LLP in Cincinnati, Ohio. I'm also a mom of two beautiful but quite unruly girls, a community and bar leader, a speaker, the founder of the Brilliant Legal Mind blog, and, oh yeah, a mindfulness and compassion teacher.

Now, you may be wondering about that last part. It's sort of a "one of these things is not like the other" situation, isn't it? Trust me, I get it, but it's all true. I came to mindfulness and compassion the old-fashioned way: I fell apart and had to learn how to put myself back together.

Though I have now had a successful practice at small and midsize firms for more than fourteen years, I nearly quit early in my law practice. I struggled with anxiety, depression, and overthinking for most of my life, and these habits only got worse when I started practicing law. At first, perfectionism helped me make my billable hours goals, but eventually I was forced to reckon with the fact that I had no skills for managing stress and no self-compassion.

Fortunately, my entire life changed for the better when I learned about compassion. And when I say "learned about,"

I don't mean that I took a class. I learned about compassion from experiencing firsthand what it meant to live without it. In my first few years of law practice, my world was turned upside down when I confronted an issue that I couldn't solve with study and hard work: my first baby was diagnosed with IUGR ("intrauterine growth restricted").

This meant I had three months of a reduced work schedule with extra medical appointments, three weeks of bed rest to do nothing but worry, and an induced labor at thirty-seven weeks. Though my baby girl was born healthy, she was only five pounds and couldn't breastfeed. While I was fortunate to work at an understanding firm, I was terrified that my law practice would never recover.

For many women, this might not be catastrophic. But for me it was devastating. After a lifetime as a perfectionist and overachiever, I couldn't do the most important thing in my life: grow and feed my baby. Rather than face the shame and pain of this, I tried to work towards redemption by pumping around the clock despite my fatigue and the clear signs of postpartum depression. I didn't stop this until my mother (a family lawyer) intervened, drove me to the doctor, and told me I had to get treatment for postpartum depression.

After a few weeks, I stabilized, my daughter ended up doing great with bottles, and she grew up fine and healthy. But that experience woke me up because I realized I could not be a good mom by treating every problem like a legal case. I had to develop some better skills for addressing human problems, and I soon started a meditation practice that changed my life.

At first, it helped me slow down. Then it helped me stop thinking all the time. But most importantly, it helped me learn how to love myself, and in turn, that helped me learn to treat other people, including my family, strangers, opposing counsel, and clients, with more warmth and kindness. Though I started out as a scared associate and a fledgling mom who got off to a rocky start, the dynamic duo of mindfulness and compassion helped me build confidence, trace the path to partnership in my law firm, and manage my life and family while doing so.

When you have an experience like that, you feel compelled to share it. So I did. Though I was nervous that people might think I was weird, my friend and coach convinced me to speak at an upcoming regional summit for women professionals. She told me, "Claire, if it helped you so much, imagine how many other people it could help." I believed strongly in the practices, so I gave it a shot.

As it turns out, my coach was right. It did help people. I spoke to two standing-room-only audiences at the summit. Women ran up to me after the sessions to tell me that they finally understood what mindfulness meant or they couldn't believe how good loving-kindness practice felt. I was quickly asked to convert my talk into a CLE for lawyers. By now, I've spoken to thousands of lawyers, paralegals, judges, and other professionals across the country in law firms, bar associations, and companies on mindfulness, compassion, stress management, and more.

Notably, however, I have done this while my law practice has not just progressed but thrived. As all of this was occurring, I advanced to partner, established my reputation as a bar and thought leader, and added new clients and practice areas to my repertoire. Even the COVID-19 pandemic did not stop the progress. Though I faced anxiety and worry like anyone, my meditation practice helped me remain stable. I eventually saw the boredom and endless time at home as an opportunity instead of a curse.

Seeing how great the mental health needs were during the pandemic, I used social distancing as a time to build skills. I obtained a meditation teacher certification from the Mindfulness Center, a 500-hour yoga teacher certification from My Vinyasa Practice, and a Compassion Educator certification from the Compassion Education Alliance. I then founded the Brilliant Legal Mind blog to share some of my learnings, resources, and meditations with other lawyers. More recently, I authored the forthcoming children's book, *Mommy Needs a Minute*, so that kids can understand the value of mindfulness and self-care for both us and them.

I know that this sounds like a lot. In truth, it sometimes feels like a lot. People ask me all of the time how I "do it all." Sometimes I say, "I don't do it all; I have help." Sometimes I say, "I don't do it all at once." Sometimes I say, "Writing helps me clean out my mind, and teaching mindfulness and compassion helps me clean out my soul." Those answers aren't wrong.

But the real answer is that I've learned to get comfortable with handling a lot, living a sometimes messy life, trying new things even when I am scared, and figuring out how to make things work. Mindfulness and compassion are the things that helped me do this, and they still help me today.

I wrote this book because I know lawyers like you have so much to offer the world. You deserve to feel good, to see what a badass you can be, and to see how the world benefits from your gifts. Mindfulness and compassion can sometimes be challenging to learn, so I wrote this book as an easy-to-read and useful resource for fellow lawyers who want to cultivate a kinder, more resilient, and happier life in the law.

Keep reading, and please subscribe to the blog at www. brilliantlegalmind.com for more information and resources about mindfulness and compassion for lawyers.

PART I
THE BASICS

Chapter 1
WHAT IS A BADASS LAWYER? (AND WHY YOU WANT TO BE ONE)

Chapter Summary:

- A badass lawyer is one who loves, trusts, cares for, and honors themselves as they serve the needs of clients.
- You don't have to change who you are to become a badass lawyer. You only need to learn to trust yourself. I'll show you how.
- With these skills, you can bring kindness into even the most difficult situations and take better care of yourself amid the stresses of law practice.

I cannot impress upon you enough how much of a nerd I am. I have no tattoos or piercings. I hate ripped jeans. I enjoy parties but generally prefer to spend my hours at home reading, writing, or cooking. I was voted most studious in high school and was the 5th grade Scrabble champion. I have made more friends through sheer awkwardness than any other personality trait. And, oh yeah, I became obsessed with the practice of sitting quietly and doing nothing so much that I wrote this book for you.

But—make no mistake—I am a badass. With this book, I hope you will see that you are a badass, too. Though this term is often used to refer to those unicorns out there who make the world better for all of us, this should not be an exclusive club. The legal profession doesn't need a secret society like the Illuminati to change for the better. It needs as many of us as it can possibly get to enlist in the work of loving ourselves, so we can take better care of each other.

When you just read "loving ourselves," a record scratch sound might have gone off in your mind like in any cheesy comedy when someone makes a horrible faux pas at a party. *Wait, what?* you may be thinking, saying to yourself, "I want to be a badass, not a sweetheart. What in the great blue blazes does loving myself have to do with practicing law?"

I get those concerns because I used to live with them. But I'm here to show you that it has everything to do with practicing law.

At its heart, law practice is about problem-solving. Whether they are looking for positive transformation or dealing with a setback, our clients always come to us in a state of crisis. Good or bad, there's always some issue that they bring us to solve, which can set their lives or businesses off in a new direction. This is hard, scary work, and not just because the stakes are high for our clients but because we, as lawyers, are our product. In contracts class in law school, we read all those cases about the sale of widgets, but our widgets are our minutes and hours and the work product of our brains.

Many of us can get the idea from law school, or maybe reading one too many dry lawyer LinkedIn profiles, that our essential value as attorneys is what we know and the results we can get. Sadly, this misses a huge part of the equation. Clients don't merely want a means to an end. They also want peace of mind. In this way, our value as lawyers depends on our ability to connect with our clients authentically so that they can trust us enough to communicate their needs and desires.

How does badassery factor in with this? Isn't this basic human stuff? Don't we learn this by the time we finish kindergarten?

Sometimes this may be true. Culturally, though, many lawyers unlearn the basic human lessons we learned as infants by the time we get out of law school. The truth is that, although emotion, connection, and vulnerability are essential to a happy life as a human, many lawyers remain uncomfortable with these things and may even attempt to hide them from view.

Think about it. What are the words you see most often on law firm websites? What words do your friends use to describe the lawyers they are looking for when they ask for a referral? In general, those words are effective, knowledgeable, experienced, or even aggressive.

Even though most experienced attorneys understand that relationships and trust are essential to law practice, it's easy to overcorrect and present in a way that hides your humanity. This can make life as a lawyer feel stifled, lonely, and dull or, in the more severe cases, lead to depression, anxiety, and substance abuse for individuals and dysfunction, harassment, and discrimination in firms and organizations.

This is why I am calling on you to be a badass. To do this, you may need to rebel against your programming by responding to stress and difficulty in a totally new way.

Let me be clear: I am not suggesting that the lawyer well-being crisis would end if we all started to behave like Saul Goodman. I'm not asking you to rebel against ethical standards or the rule of law. We've had too many lawyers and even judges who have publicly shamed the profession by abusing client relationships, blatantly violating the law, or even advocating for others to do so. These lawyers don't only damage the perception of the profession by outsiders, they also damage how lawyers view themselves and their work.

Instead, I am asking you to honor your ethical obligations as an attorney and help restore reverence for the rule of law by honoring yourself. First and foremost, this means honoring every part of you, including your messy emotions and frail and fickle body. While this can be hard and scary, badass lawyers don't run from the mess; they run towards it.

Honoring yourself also means embracing your inner wisdom. This includes listening to how you feel and letting your heart be soft instead of hardening it against the jagged edges of life. In this way, being a badass lawyer means reconnecting with your body and opening your heart, so you can tap into your intrinsic goodness.

If you are rolling your eyes right now, that's okay. I know I'm saying something that most other meditation teachers would never say to a bunch of lawyers, but trusting your intrinsic goodness is the best way to live a better, happier life.

You're allowed to be skeptical about this. Maybe for religious or other reasons, you fear that assuming your own goodness is the pavement on the primrose path to hell. But you don't have to always presume that you are doing good or never reflect to consider if the impact of your actions is good.

My point here is more fundamental. I'm suggesting that a badass lawyer is someone who knows what feels good because they have paid attention, knows how to get back to good whenever it seems lost or hidden, and trusts in their capacity to bring good into any situation, even when it just means being present.

This is the way that you can transform your life and law practice.

No matter how bad the situation is, you will be less concerned with looking good and can focus more on doing good. This is what will make your work invaluable to clients and the world at large. A lawyer who can trust themself is one who can see the situation clearly, remove their ego from the equation, and do the work that needs to be done, even when it is scary, frustrating, or hard. They can do this without sacrificing themselves on the altar of achievement because they know how to honor and care for themselves even in the face of hardship.

Even more importantly, I'm here to tell you that change is possible for you. It's even possible with practices that take only a few minutes each day.

It's fair to be skeptical. You may know too many lawyers who have let the profession change them. You may know too many stories of people whose work as lawyers drove them to mental health crises, drugs or alcohol, or persistent and visible unhappiness.

I don't deny that those stories exist. In fact, I have lived that story myself. As a young lawyer, I tried to deal with all problems in my life like a lawyer: by doing my research and working as hard as I possibly could. When my first daughter was born small and couldn't breastfeed, I tried to learn all the tricks to get her to latch on and worked around the clock to pump and try to feed her.

All the while, I ignored how bad I felt, how tired I was, and how little I cared if she thrived on breastmilk or formula. It only took a few weeks to see that work can't fix every problem and that I couldn't survive without treating myself with kindness.

Why does this story matter? It matters because mindfulness and compassion helped me change, and research shows I am not alone.

That experience was one of the worst times in my life, but I see it as a gift now because it shook me out of my all-too-human, but nonetheless wrongheaded, worldview that work and achievement were the way to happiness. After sleep, family support, and therapy helped me heal from that experience, I started a meditation practice that changed my life and saved my law practice.

It helped me make peace with my overactive mind and start to understand and practice self-kindness. Over time, that turned into far more active and courageous kindness towards others and greater comfort in simply being myself. Within a few years, my law practice, on the verge of extinction, transformed into a thriving and happy one.

I don't dare to presume that mindfulness and compassion are the only things needed to transform the lives of so many lawyers struggling with wellness today. In fact, I wouldn't claim that my own life changed because I meditated. To be sure, my life didn't change until I started living it differently, by asking for and accepting help, responding to my challenges with kindness instead of judgment, and facing risks and adversity instead of freezing up, dodging them, or running from them.

Here's the thing, though: You may not know how to change your life for the better until you start paying close attention to how you behave.

Even if you want to change your life, you may not know how to get outside of your thoughts, treat yourself kindly, or trust your body. Those are the skills you will learn in this book. You will discover how to find your breath and use it as a tool, so you can bring calm with you anywhere. You will cultivate comfort with your body and understanding of your emotions. And you will practice kindness for yourself and gentleness with others even when life makes those things hard.

I hope you've picked up on it by now that being a badass lawyer does not require you to change yourself at all. You don't need to train or even read this book to be a badass lawyer. You already are a badass lawyer. With this book, I hope to help you see that and unlock it.

The world and the legal profession will not change with meditation alone. So, I didn't write this book just to get you to meditate. I wrote this book to give you a simple, relatable, and practicable explanation of mindfulness and compassion so that you can put these time-tested, research-based tools to work in your life and law practice. In short, I didn't write this book because I thought it would change the world. I wrote it for all of you badass lawyers so that you can change the world.

- What Do You Think?

Take a moment and think about what brought you here. What made you want to read this book? What skills are you interested in building in your life? What viewpoints do you want to consider? What change do you want to see happen in your life or the world? Consider these ideas or even write a few paragraphs about them in your journal.

- Next Steps

I have given you my thoughts on what a badass lawyer is, but as lawyers, we know that definitions of terms do not tell the full story. Most of us need case examples to help us understand how a concept or rule plays out in the real world. To understand this concept better, take a moment and consider or write about the following ideas:

- Identify people from history or your life who you would consider badasses. What about them did you find most inspiring?
- Identify times in your life when you felt like a badass. What about those situations made you feel proud?
- Think about the common themes running through all these examples.
- Consider how these traits might benefit your life, law practice, or the world today.

To learn more about mindfulness and compassion and what it offers to lawyers, subscribe to the blog at www.brilliantlegalmind.com.

What are your thoughts or insights?

CHAPTER 2
WHAT IS COMPASSION? (HINT: IT'S WAY MORE THAN BEING NICE)

Chapter Summary:

- Compassion (vs. empathy, which leads to burnout) is the ability to stay with suffering (any difficulty in life) while maintaining the willingness to help.

- Lawyers deal with client problems and the challenges of law practice every day, so compassion cultivation can help lawyers take better care of themselves as they do their jobs.

- Although compassion is an innate human response that most of us experience naturally, it can be blocked by habit, cultural messages, past trauma, or stress.

- For this reason, the intentional cultivation of compassion for oneself and others is a practical necessity for lawyers.

Take a moment to envision a cave. It's barren, spacious, dark, cold, and hard. Now, imagine that you have lived your entire life in this cave. You can't escape the cave. The best you can do is that sometimes you get visitors who may brighten up the cave or at least offer a temporary distraction. But, when they leave, it's just you left in the cave to sit and sleep on the hard stone floor in the cold and dark.

Now, imagine that suddenly you find a little fire in the cave. It provides light and warmth. Suddenly you can see how beautiful the rock formations on the wall are, and you are no longer shivering with cold. Then, a comfortable couch appears, and a vibrant and soft throw rug on the floor. You now have a soft place to rest, and it feels a bit easier to greet visitors with joy and enthusiasm when they visit. Regardless of which visitors come to you, good or bad, when they leave, at least you have a relatively comfortable place to rest.

If I asked you which living arrangement you'd prefer, hands down you would tell me option two, right? Would you be surprised to know, however, that lots of lawyers implicitly choose to reside in option one for most of our lives? If you haven't figured it out yet, the cave that I am talking about above is no more real than the cave Plato talked about to prove his point about human nature.

Much like that allegorical cave, this one is an analogy for your mind. I'm using this analogy here to help you understand how the innate and foundational capacities of mindfulness and compassion work together.

Our beautiful human minds have some inherent capacities. One is mindfulness, or the capacity to be nonjudgmentally aware in the present moment of our thoughts and sensory perceptions. Many lawyers now know about mindfulness. Research tells us how it can help you manage stress, improve focus, increase happiness, and even treat physical and mental health conditions. Although mindfulness has this amazing potential, in isolation, it's similar to cave number one. It's nothing more than a latent capacity to receive information.

You may be wondering why mindfulness is getting such good press when cave number one doesn't sound that appealing. That's because when researchers and meditation teachers are telling you to meditate, they aren't just talking about mindfulness alone.

Normally, they are talking about mindfulness plus compassion. Due to the frenetic style of modern life, mindfulness is emphasized because just getting some present-moment awareness can be an everyday struggle for most lawyers. Having meditated and taught mindfulness for years now, however, real personal development with mindfulness happens when you cultivate not just awareness but kindness too.

When I talk about compassion in this book, I am talking about the difference between living in cave number one and cave number two. Just like the cozy fire, fuzzy throw rug, and comfy couch, compassion is the soft and comforting stuff that works with basic awareness to make life worth living. Just like mindfulness, on the other hand, it is a capacity that can be cultivated with training.

So what is compassion, and why is it so important?

Researchers define compassion as the capacity to stay present with the experience of suffering, whether our own or others, and remain willing to help. Any of you who have spent the night next to a loved one in the hospital or placed a Band-Aid on the knee of a wailing child may think that this is human nature. As I said, it is human nature. It's something we are all wired to do and to need because without this capacity to care our species wouldn't have lasted this long.

However, this is not the only possible response. The human stress response can and often does block compassion. When our bodies perceive a threat, a chain reaction occurs that can induce the fight/flight/freeze reaction. Our midbrain takes over and often directs us to attack the threat, get away from it, or do nothing. In other words, the stress response to threats can make it difficult for us to stay present, let alone remain willing to help.

This is why cultivating mindfulness and compassion can be so transformational. It can be like redecorating your inner living conditions to make them more hospitable.

When your mind cave is more comfortable, you can see things more clearly and feel safer and more supported to handle whatever guests may arise on your doorstep. With this added level of comfort, you may find yourself able to greet the welcome guests (all the nice experiences in life) with genuine joy and engagement and the less welcome guests (all the nasty experiences in life) with kindness and curiosity.

Words like kindness and curiosity are soft and evoke the image of a child, but don't get the wrong impression with this. This ability is a superpower in real life. Sure, kindness is gentle, but it isn't just nice. When we cultivate compassion, we aren't training the mind to see life through rose-colored lenses or escape to a happy place when life is too much.

I'm talking about the opposite. I'm talking about greeting the nasty parts of life, the nasty people in life, and the nasty parts of ourselves with kindness. Surely you can see how this is exceptionally difficult, incredibly brave, and exactly what many lawyers, if not people across the world, need right now.

This can create a huge shift in the way that you live and practice law, and it doesn't have to take a lot of your time each day.

If you are anything like me, you were raised to be competitive, protective, and perhaps even argumentative. Law practice often validates those habits, so they get stronger. Over time, they can cause you to lose touch with how you feel and how you make other people feel. Mindfulness and compassion training can help you undo that process to reconnect with how kindness feels and learn to use it in your law practice. By reducing judgment, getting more comfortable in your body, and developing strategies to calm and soothe the body and tend to your emotions, you will build comfort with the hard parts of life.

Perhaps you have heard the term "compassion fatigue" used to describe the plight of lawyers and others in service professions. You may be wondering why I am talking about compassion as a positive thing when it has harmed so many in our profession.

There is a critical distinction here between empathy and compassion that you need to understand.

The term "compassion fatigue" has been used by smart people with undoubtedly good intentions, but it is a misnomer. What many refer to as compassion fatigue is what many leading minds, including the phenomenal Brené Brown and the brilliant Dr. Judson Brewer, author of *The Craving Mind*, call "empathic overwhelm." Unlike compassion, empathy can be quickly overwhelmed and fatigued.

Empathy is the ability to feel what others are feeling. Though it underlies the compassion response, it lacks the willingness to help and is self-focused. Thus, where empathy can be isolating, become overwhelmed, and trigger a threat response, compassion builds connections to others, protects us so that we can act, and rewards us. While compassion often arises amid a stress response, the body rewards the desire to help with a release of the love hormones (including serotonin, oxytocin, and dopamine) that may induce euphoria, satisfaction, or feelings of well-being.

Because compassion and empathy are closely related, most of us may need to consciously cultivate compassion so that it is there for us when we need it. This is not so much a call to change our inherent personalities or encouragement to be less aggressive in our strategies.

The point here is that the cultivation of mindfulness with compassion can help you respond to stress in a new way, get better results in your law practice, and be happier in the process.

Though it can be hard to believe, a softer approach can be stronger even in law practice. My first inclination in many situations is to fight, but I have gotten better results when I try a new approach. Years ago, I was in settlement negotiations with an attorney with whom I did not enjoy a very good working relationship. Both parties professed an interest in resolution, but our email exchanges drove us further apart. My partner and I were aghast that our appeals to logic could not close the deal.

Instead of responding with another email, I saw what my opposing counsel couldn't say explicitly: They struggled to respond rationally because they were offended by our settlement offer. I could have judged them for letting their feelings affect the case (a mortal but common sin for most lawyers). Instead, I took a breath and saw another truth: My relationship with opposing counsel would continue to cause problems if I didn't work to fix it. I also saw that, even if I didn't intend offense, it was easy for lawyers to feel attacked in settlement negotiations.

After taking a moment to walk in my opponent's shoes, I made the brave choice to pick up the phone. I told opposing counsel that my client genuinely wanted to settle the case, and I apologized if I had said or done anything to offend them in the past. The same opposing counsel who had written hostile emails to me only minutes before expressed gratitude and appreciation for the call. Within a few days, the case was settled.

Of course, this story isn't a promise that compassion can get all of your cases settled. It shows, however, that mindfulness and compassion are courageous, powerful, and useful in law practice.

As I said earlier, compassion is the ability to stay with the experience of difficulty and maintain the willingness to help. In the example above, I had to stay present with my frustration, the rancor of opposing counsel, and any external pressure to get good results for my client. I could have fought against this by continuing to argue via email, fled by ignoring the emails, or checked out by giving up on the process. It was the presence of this difficulty and the willingness to look at the situation with kindness and curiosity that even opened the possibility of helping.

It also felt a whole lot better. After that experience with opposing counsel, I can't claim that we ever became close friends. Like all adversaries, we had spats about documents, evidentiary issues, and case schedules. However, we were able to develop a working relationship from that point on and understood each other better. I also felt proud for bringing my personality and problem-solving abilities to my practice in a way that clearly benefited my client. Though I like winning and feeling dominant about as much as any litigator out there, it's also exciting to feel powerful, steady, and supported because of your ability to collaborate.

Given how stressful and busy the legal profession is, you may need to make a concerted effort to strengthen these skills to support your law practice.

Just like I was, you may be living in cave number one as your default setting because your iPhone can be a cruel mistress, and you have too little time for things like kindness, let alone self-care.

Fortunately, the practices in this book do not require a large investment of time each day. Instead, they only require an open mind and the courage to begin opening your heart. With a little bit of consistency and a whole lot of self-kindness, you will be amazed to see how much you can change your inner landscape and how that, in turn, changes how you view and relate to the rest of the world.

- What Do You Think?

Now that you know more about what compassion means and what it may offer to you as a lawyer, I invite you to think about ways that kindness has affected your law practice. Are there any times when a softer approach has helped you move a case forward? Are there any times in your work when it took courage to use a softer approach? How did those experiences feel at the time, and how did you feel after you experienced them?

- Next Steps

As a practice, take a moment to consider your mental cave. Can you describe how it looks and feels? You can write this out, draw a picture, create a collage, or simply sit for a moment and consider how your mind feels to you. Notice how your mind feels right now in this moment, or think more broadly about how your mind feels most of the time. As you do this, feel free to consider if there are any ways that you could begin to make your mental cave more hospitable.

If you want to understand compassion more and explore practices designed for lawyers, subscribe to the blog at www. brilliantlegalmind.com.

What are your thoughts or insights?

Chapter 3

The "Secret" Recipe That Can Make Lawyers True Badasses

Chapter Summary:

- Compassion is a dynamic process, often involving the mind, body, and heart.
- To cultivate compassion, it is useful to explore its mental, emotional, and physical aspects individually.
- Learning the skills individually will also help you manage overthinking, understand your emotions, and recognize and care for your physical signs of stress.
- When each aspect is explored individually, you will be ready to put them together to do loving-kindness practice and ultimately use compassion in your law practice and life.

In the last chapter, I painted a picture of a cozy cave to demonstrate the difference between mindfulness and compassion. That made me think of Mr. Tumnus from *The Chronicles of Narnia: The Lion, the Witch, and the Wardrobe* or maybe Piglet from *Winnie the Pooh*. Fortunately, those characters are awesome examples of compassion, and one of the ways they showed it was through food. Mr. Tumnus invited Lucy and company into his cave for a meal to fortify them on their journey to the Stone Table. Piglet, as we know, shared all kinds of meals and picnics with his bud, Winnie.

Maybe it was reading all these stories of awesome meals growing up, but I have loved cooking since I was a kid. I quickly outgrew my Easy Bake Oven and started experimenting with my mom's old Betty Crocker cookbook from the 1950s. The first recipe I ever made was a peanut butter and jelly sandwich.

Now, I had made a PB&J before, but I was not practicing how to make a sandwich. Instead, I used the book to learn how to follow a recipe. Having now cooked for over thirty years, I can make far more complicated dishes like Julia Child's famous coq au vin. I can even make up dishes on the fly without cracking a book. It's because, over the years, I have practiced and played at cooking so much that it's a skill ingrained in me that I can use whenever needed.

This example is useful here because, in many ways, mindfulness and compassion are like cooking. Much like cooking, most of us have some basic capacities, but training and practice can make the capacities even stronger.

Most humans can do basic food preparations without training. Just like a PB&J sandwich, even our innate mindfulness and compassion are nourishing and excellent. In the same way, however, we can train mindfulness and compassion skills to make a new and amazing dish out of life with whatever ingredients come our way.

How do we do this? What is the recipe for cultivating mindfulness and compassion? As I explained, compassion is the response to suffering, which means that stress will normally be involved. Though we can't guarantee any particular response, we can understand the mind, body, and heart better to let mindfulness and compassion flow. Because the stress response is a dynamic process of the mind and body, it may help us to separate out the processes and examine each part before we can put it all together.

In this way, it is not dissimilar to mixing the wet and dry ingredients separately first before you combine them to make cookie dough. Over the last ten years, I've broken down, examined, recombined, and used these aspects in my meditation practice, teacher training, and in my law practice.

My old family recipe for mindfulness and compassion cultivation for lawyers is:

1. Establish mindfulness of thoughts
2. Foster body awareness
3. Consciously reconnect with kindness

In the chapters that follow, we will explore each aspect and try practices that can help you build a foundation in these critical ingredients. At the end, I will show you how you can combine them back together to bring mindfulness and compassion into your law practice and life. By the end of the book, my goal is that you will not just pick up a few new meditation strategies that you can use at your next retreat. Instead, my goal is that you will have a better sense of how you can let compassion flow more naturally in your life, law practice, and the world.

The results from harnessing the power of mindfulness and compassion in your life can be truly life changing.

I've already told you how, early in my law practice, I started meditating to get relief from overthinking and anxiety. Well, the rubber really started to meet the road for me when I found loving-kindness practice, which we'll explore in Chapter 7. It quickly became the practice I relied on after dark days in my law practice, where I had to deal with a difficult witness in a deposition all day or got a bad result in a case.

Positive affirmations (i.e., "I am peaceful," "I am loved," "I am powerful and strong," etc.) always made my mind go haywire with objections (i.e., "Oh really?" "Then why don't they help with the dishes?" "Ha! Not feeling it now," etc.). Loving-kindness practice, on the other hand, short-circuited this mental chatter because it bypassed my brain and went straight to my heart. It helped me remember not only the people I loved but also what love felt like. Doing the practice didn't make the problems go away, but it reminded me that I was never alone in facing them. Even on the hardest days, it made me feel peaceful, loved, powerful, and strong.

When I speak to lawyers and law firms, I always recommend practices like loving-kindness that encourage compassion cultivation.

For someone like me, the practice made all the difference in the world. If any of the following sounds familiar to you, compassion practices can probably help you too. I had always been lost in my thoughts, disconnected from my body, and I prized my resourcefulness and self-reliance. When a problem in life arose, my first instinct was to think the issue through to come up with some perfect solution. Unfortunately, this would lead to overthinking because I was trying to do the impossible: outsmart life.

Of course, scheming never revealed to me the way to make life and law practice simple and neat, and I always ended up feeling lost, weak, and stuck. Early in my practice, I felt like a failure almost every day because I didn't know what I was doing as a new mom, struggled with my litigation practice, and had no earthly idea how I would build a book of business to advance to partner.

For a long time, I was lost in shame, fear, loneliness, and self-doubt. Meditation helped me early on because it gave me relief from the spiraling thoughts and helped me manage the physical aspects of my stress.

I learned the hard way that focusing on my breath was not enough, so I want to help you learn in an easier and quicker way that practices for the body and heart are essential too.

Like most new meditators, I started out by focusing on my breath and returning to it when my mind wandered. I don't knock this time-tested and research-proven practice, and you'll learn about and try it in Chapter 4. I'm lucky, though, that one of the first teachers to influence my practice was Tara Brach, a trained psychologist who emphasized body awareness and self-kindness. When I heard her repeatedly say on her podcast that there wasn't anything wrong with me, something clicked for me. I started to realize that the answer to my problem was a lack of kindness.

For most of my life until that point, I had always looked at difficulty as a weakness, seen mistakes as products of an inherent character flaw, and believed, albeit unconsciously, that the path to finding and showing love was through achievement. Nobody ever said this to me, but I got so much validation for my achievements that I forgot that real love is there no matter what we do.

Here's why this is important. Lots of people try meditation because they want to feel peaceful, but some never get to the practices like loving-kindness that go directly to the source of peace: love, kindness, and connection.

When I started doing loving-kindness practice, I went right to the source and found the peace I was seeking. I got to experience love all by itself and for no reason at all. From sending love to myself regularly, I saw the truth that love was not just the consequence of good action but a necessary precondition for it.

When I sent love to friends and family, I understood in a new way how deeply they mattered to me such that the barriers I had allowed to build in my life seemed to no longer make any sense. I even saw how I could send love out to my broader community and the world at large for no reason at all. The practice reminded me that love and kindness have inherent value and that it is our birthright as humans to participate in and experience them.

When I teach lawyers about this, I know that some may be skeptical. If I am being honest, though, I love changing their minds about how powerful compassion can be.

I know it may seem counterintuitive that power can come from the softest and gooiest of our emotions, but it's true. Loving-kindness practice not only made my meditation practice more robust and sustainable, it totally transformed my life and law practice.

First, it helped me acknowledge with kindness that I was lonely, and that allowed me to make a concerted effort to reach out to make new friends and build a community of supporters. Increased kindness created confidence to pursue things outside billable hours, including writing, speaking, and networking activities. Finally, the quieting of my thinking mind and judgment allowed me to take risks in life by applying for awards, speaking opportunities, and taking on leadership roles in and outside of my firm.

All these things took courage and required me to manage my time, energy, and emotions, but over the course of a few years, I went from feeling like a failure to winning awards, making partner, and becoming a thought leader in the profession.

You may be even more surprised to know that all of these amazing results happened, not in a life full of ease but in one checkered with adversity and setbacks.

The achievements I listed above are good examples of how mindfulness and compassion can help you transform your life even when life is hard. While I was experiencing all this change I:

- lost two close family members in the span of a week
- faced mental health challenges in my family
- experienced marital difficulties
- managed change, turnover, and dissension in my law firm
- experienced a traumatic and totally unexpected emergency C-section during the birth of my second daughter
- lived and managed a law practice through the COVID-19 pandemic

Don't get me wrong here. I'm not saying that mindfulness and compassion practices cause personal transformation because they will change the fundamental reality that life is hard. Nothing can do that.

What I am saying is that mindfulness and compassion can improve your life because they can change how you relate to it.

For me, the practices helped me face and handle all the scary, angsty, nasty bits of life so that I felt strong enough, brave enough, and energetic enough to not just survive the rest of my life but grow and build more on top of it. This is the badassery I want you to experience, too, because you deserve it, and the world needs it.

One thing about the lawyer well-being problem that drives me nuts is the fact that lawyers trained to take on and solve the problems of the world are unwell, unhappy, and, in many cases, addicted. It seems like the ultimate cruel joke, doesn't it? We train for three years, if not more, to help other people with their problems, but in many cases, we seem unable to handle our own.

I'm here to tell you that we aren't unable to handle our problems. We have everything we need to handle our problems and more if we go back to square one and teach ourselves how to read the recipe for personal development and building a happy life.

Law school taught us how to think about the law and use it to our client's advantage, but it perhaps may have caused many of us to forget the basics of happiness: love, connection, health, and safety. In the following chapters, we will go step-by-step through practices to help you reconnect with these essential ingredients, so you can learn to use the recipe of happiness and well-being for yourself.

- What Do You Think?

I realize that I opened a chapter on generating badassery with a reference to Piglet from *Winnie the Pooh*, so I get it if you are feeling a bit skeptical right now. Skeptical is fine because at least it means you are paying attention. However, let's not have that skepticism harden into judgment just yet. If you have some reactions to these ideas, take a moment to identify them. What exactly are you skeptical or unsure about? Or, in the alternative, if you love an idea I discussed, what is particularly appealing to you? Whether good or bad, examining your reactions here may help you explore the topics more deeply as we continue.

- Next Steps

In this chapter, we talked about the recipe for letting mindfulness and compassion flow, which we will explore more in the next part of the book. As we'll discuss more later, a fundamental aspect of this is kindness, or an open, nonjudgmental awareness. Think for yourself for a moment about what kindness means to you.

Searching a dictionary or writing your personal definition is great, but I encourage you to consider the meaning of kindness in other ways too. Envision a recent experience of kindness, whether you were offering or receiving it, and notice what happens in your mind and body as you do. Take a few minutes to write out your experience afterward or jot down the few most prominent ideas that come to mind.

For more resources to help you envision what mindfulness and compassion look like in the life of a practicing lawyer, subscribe to the blog at www.brilliantlegalmind.com.

What are your thoughts or insights?

PART II
Easily Building the Foundational Skills of Mindfulness and Compassion

Chapter 4

Step 1: Establishing Presence (by Doing Lots of Things You Already Know)

Chapter Summary:

- Mindfulness is our capacity for present moment awareness without judgment.

- Though all of us experience mindfulness, most of us need to practice it to build the skill of nonjudgmental awareness.

- Breath practice, or using the breath as a focal point in meditation, is one of the most common and effective ways to engender the cultivation of mindfulness.

- The point of this practice, or any other mindfulness practice, is not to be good at it but instead to notice what is there without reaction.

- Potential benefits of mindfulness practice include increased focus (i.e., less trailing off during critical conversations), calm and stability (i.e., staying centered during difficult conversations), and greater awareness of one's habits of mind and personality tendencies (i.e., noticing overthinking or the tendency towards perfectionism).

Now that we've explored what compassion is and what it offers to lawyers, it's time to start digging in with the practices to begin exploring each aspect of our compassion response. The first ingredient to compassion is mindfulness. Recall the definition of compassion that I offered in Chapter 2: presence with difficulty and the willingness to help. Mindfulness is presence.

The mind is not wired to stay present for long, even in the best circumstances. The threat response to stress can make presence even harder in difficult circumstances. If you have ever felt like your thoughts are scattered or had difficulty focusing, it may have been the normal functioning of the mind in the midst of a stress response. Though this situation is normal, it can be frustrating.

The good news is that the cultivation of mindfulness can help. So, what is mindfulness?

There are many definitions for the term, but I prefer the definition from one of the researchers who made mindfulness a household term, Jon Kabat-Zinn. He defines mindfulness as "awareness that arises through paying attention, on purpose, in the present moment, non-judgmentally."

Put another way, this means intentionally paying attention to what's happening right now without reacting to or evaluating the experience. As I said in Chapter 2, mindfulness is more of a trait than a state. It's a capacity to receive information, and that's why I analogized it to an empty cave.

Many of us associate mindfulness with meditation, but they are not the same. Meditation is a practice that can lead to more mindfulness in one's life, and that, in turn, can lead to better focus, more happiness, and less stress. You don't have to meditate to be mindful, but most of us need to practice building a foundation in mindfulness because of the way our brains work and how busy our lives are. For most of us, the best way to do this is to get started with meditation.

THE BASIC BREATH PRACTICE

The most common method that teachers offer new meditators is the practice of following one's breath. I will refer to this practice throughout the book as breath practice. In this style, you will find a comfortable and stable position[1] and bring your attention to the breath. You can do this in a variety of ways. I prefer to focus on the feelings of the breath coming and going out of my body at my belly, but focusing on the breath at the nostrils, throat, or chest is fine too. Another way to focus on the breath is to note the cycle of inhales and exhales as they occur.

Regardless of how you focus on the breath, the practice is to count each breath, starting at one and ending at five or ten, and then start the counting over again at the end. When your mind wanders, and it certainly will, the practice is to simply return your attention back to your breath. Designate a period of time you wish to sit, set a timer, and then do this process for the duration.

---

[1] You will notice that I don't spend too much time in this book discussing meditation posture. That's because I have meditated every way, from sitting, to standing, walking, or even lying down. Any posture is okay, but what you really need is something that is safe, stable, and comfortable enough to allow you to focus. I wouldn't stress about this, but it may help you to monitor what works for you and what doesn't. If you want more on posture, *Zen Mind Beginner's Mind* by Shunryo Suzuki has a lot about that and a lot of other wisdom.

Why Breath Practice Is Important

Now, you may be wondering, *Why on Earth has so much been said about a practice as simple as that?* In truth, breath practice is quite basic, but it is basic in the sense that it is fundamental. You may go your whole life without noticing it, but your breath is an important link between your body and mind.

Recall the discussion of the stress response in Chapter 1. When a threat exists, your body and mind can initiate a stress response that includes an increase in your heart and breath rate. So, one way to calm yourself and return to neutral is to soothe and calm the body. When you focus deliberately on your breath, especially the exhale, your mind sends a signal to the body that you are safe and have plenty of oxygen. This is why we all tell each other to "take a breath" when agitation arises.

Of course, it would be the rare person who could immediately stop a stress response to threats in one breath.

Many of us may be shallow breathers or may not be accustomed to paying attention to our breath. Merely taking a breath or even a few breaths in the state of upheaval may not therefore be sufficient. Beyond this, you may be bombarded by thoughts, emotions, and physical sensations as you experience stress that can perpetuate the agitation and impede calming down.

That's why most of us need to practice working with our breath. By practice, however, I don't mean hours on end. As you'll read below, a few minutes a day at first is enough.

Most of us would not walk into a trial without having prepared extensively first. We all know that nervousness impedes performance, but we also know that we cannot do our best work with complicated things while learning on the fly. Thus, just like preparations get you ready for trial, meditation gets you ready for life. To use your breath as a tool to bring calm and stability into your life, it helps to first sharpen that tool and learn how to use it.

Beyond this, while I am endeavoring in this book to separate the experiences of our mind, body, and heart for the purposes of better understanding, the reality remains that these experiences are intertwined. Meditation may be the closest approximation to separating out some of these processes precisely because you slow things down, do very little, and minimize distractions. Therefore, breath practice isn't merely a tool to calm oneself. Instead, it is also a foundational practice that allows you to see what's really there in your mind, body, and heart.

LIKELY BENEFITS OF BREATH PRACTICE

If you try breath practice, the first thing you are likely to notice is that it isn't easy. During meditation, you may be frustrated, bored, confused, or feel inept. All of those things are normal, but I encourage you to keep going as long as these feelings don't get so intense that it only causes you pain. The reason for this is that the benefits of your meditation practice aren't likely to show up in the practice itself. They are more likely to show up in your life.

Early signs that your meditation practice is off to a good start include the following:

- noticing when you are thinking
- catching yourself rushing
- catching yourself drifting and coming back
- noticing when you are about to judge/react
- learning how to relax on demand

- noticing your breath (or other signs of stress) in your daily activities

You may know why these small things can be incredibly important, but I am going to say it outright just to make sure we are on the same page. These things matter because they give you a chance to make a choice. If you see that you are thinking or rushing or stressing or judging, you have the chance to stop, slow down, examine, rest, or relax.

In other words, these tiny changes open up the possibility of choosing a result that can lead to more peace, connection, kindness, happiness, or just overall better results.

DON'T WORRY ABOUT BEING GOOD AT BREATH PRACTICE

If these results can happen even early on with a meditation practice, you may be wondering why everyone doesn't do it. That's a fair question, but the answer is easy: Meditation itself is hard, and to be honest, it can be scary for most of us.

Remember my cave analogy from Chapter 2? When you start meditating, the experience may be like sitting in a cold, dark, lonely cave. You may not know what's lurking in there because you've never looked. Because the practice is new, you may not be sure you have the skills to handle what comes up. In this way, opening yourself up to the contents of your mind in meditation may feel as daunting as opening the fridge when you know it has been too long since you cleaned it out.

This is why I tell lawyers when I speak and teach not to worry about being good at meditation.

First, this means don't expect to be calm or to feel like you can easily focus without distraction. Breath practice is

fundamental, but that does not mean it is easy. It is fundamental because it goes right to the heart of the source of your
unhappiness as a human, but it does this by training your
brain to do something it doesn't want to do.

Your brain is not wired to stay focused on one thing for
long. Instead, it is wired to wander to the past or flit to fantasies about the future. By focusing on your breath, in the
here and now, you are asking your mind to stay in the present.
This is no different than asking a small child to sit still and
be quiet, so don't expect discipline and perfection right away.

Your mind is also not wired to see things as they are.
Instead, it will react internally to almost every experience
you have, and this can happen so quickly that you think
your reaction is the experience itself. When you focus on
the breath, the instruction is to focus on the breath *as it is.*
But inevitably, your mind will wonder if you are focusing
on the breath in the "right way." It will create doubts about
whether you can do the practice at all, or it will wander away
from your focal point and create reactions to your thoughts
and bodily sensations. Then you may even have reactions to
your reactions.

The point of all of this, of course, is not to make you swear
never to try meditation. Instead, it is to acknowledge that
the practice is hard. It takes courage even to be willing to sit
with yourself in silence.

It's challenging to try something your brain is wired
not to want to do. For this reason, the best way to start a
meditation practice is to drop all expectations about being
good at it and instead treat it like play, be humble, and have
a sense of humor.

It's also best to start small. I started my practice with
increments of one to two minutes at a time and added on a

minute or two as I could tolerate it. You will experience many thoughts and sensations you never noticed before when you start practicing, so it can be easy to feel overwhelmed. To be kind to yourself as you face something new and challenging, start small to allow yourself time to develop understanding and coping skills.

SKILLS YOU CAN PICK UP BY BEING BAD AT MEDITATION

I know it may be hard to imagine, but giving yourself permission to suck at meditation can be life-changing. By now, most of us have heard about the growth mindset made popular by researcher and author Carol S. Dweck. You may know that the first step to building a skill is often suffering and fumbling through a new experience.

Even if this makes sense and you can remember times in your life when mastery was borne out of awkwardness and artlessness, this experience can feel truly terrible. For lawyers, it may be even worse because we may feel a compulsion to always look like we know what we are doing.

Even so, you don't ever have to get good at breath practice to reap benefits from it.

A while ago, my daughter asked me if I was good at meditation because I had done it for so long, and I answered her honestly. I said, "No, I don't think I'll ever be good at it, but I keep doing it because it's good for me."

I have been a perfectionist my whole life, and though curious by nature, I stuck for too long to hobbies and activities I expected to be good at from the outset. Meditation may be the first thing I chose for myself where I didn't have to be good.

Once I did that and saw the results, I gave myself permission to suck at lots of other things. I started writing and speaking more, I made a concerted effort to network and be a better friend, and I even recently changed up my law practice to add some new areas. This opened up doors for me I could never have expected, and the same thing is possible for you.

In addition, even though you will inevitably be lost in thought, the past or future, or internal reactions in meditation, the practice is what will build the skills of focus, stability, and calm over time.

Each time you notice your mind wandering, it might feel frustrating, and you'll learn how to bring kindness to this experience in Chapter 6. Even so, it's actually good because noticing is the object.

If you notice where your mind is in meditation, you can also notice when your mind is churning thoughts or going into reaction mode in real life, and that may empower you to slow down and make wiser choices. Over time, you are also likely to see patterns that give you insight into your habits of mind, deep-seated fears, and inner longings. In this way, all that mind-wandering that you may be trying to avoid can help you understand yourself better.

One common example of this is doubt. Though in retrospect, I now realize that my doubt complex is strong, I was not aware of it until I started meditating. Unaware of my patterns of thought, I assumed that my doubts were the voices of reason. When I began meditating regularly, I saw how frequently doubt came up, including for things that were objectively good for me.

What this means, then, is eventually, meditation can help you see repetitive thoughts as patterns of mind instead of inherent truths.

This is how the practice of meditation can help you face destructive habits like self-doubt and take action so that they no longer hold you back. Just as Elizbeth Gilbert describes in *Big Magic,* meditation can help you make friends with habits of mind like doubt so that you can take them along for the ride but not allow them to drive.

In short, being bad at meditation doesn't point to a problem with your practice or with you. Instead, being bad at meditation is the practice. If the object is to find focus, you practice that by coming back to your focal point again and again. If the object is to establish and maintain calm, you practice that by looking for calm even when you don't feel that way. If the point is to stay present, you practice that by sitting and being present with whatever is there.

• What Do You Think?

Close your eyes and take a full deep breath. As you do, focus on how the breath feels coming in and how it feels going out. Then notice how you feel for a moment after doing so. Guess what? You just meditated. There is no rule that says meditation must be any number of breaths or any length of time. It can happen anywhere, and it is most useful when we can use it in our lives.

With that understanding in mind, take a moment to think about how you already have mindfulness in your life or things that you can do to bring more mindfulness into your life. As I have already said, I am a big fan of small gradual change, so don't overthink this or underestimate how meaningful subtle life changes can be.

• Next Steps

Try the same deep breath exercise you just did but repeat it a total of ten times. Congratulations! You just meditated for one minute. For the next seven days, keep the habit up. Add a minute every day or two until you get to five minutes (less than 0.1 hours). Feel free to use a meditation app or other guided meditations, but focus for now on mindfulness practices and avoid visualizations or heavy imagery. The goal this week is to work on building the initial skill of becoming aware when your mind wanders and starting the process of noticing your inner patterns.

If you feel inclined, you can then consider what a meditation practice might look like in your life. In the bestselling book *Atomic Habits,* James Clear tells us that our identities often affect our habits. You may not think of yourself as a meditator just yet. This exercise will help you imagine what meditation might look like for you so that your identity can expand to include it. If you want to think more deeply about how to make meditation a habit, check out the Meditation Habit Worksheet available on my blog at http://brilliantlegalmind.com/resources/meditation-habit-worksheet-2/.

What are your thoughts or insights?

Chapter 5
Step 2: Reconnecting with Your Body (to Give Your Lawyer Brain a Break)

Chapter Summary:

- Many lawyers lack body awareness due to habit or the business of contemporary life, so taking the time to notice and build comfort with bodily sensations can be helpful.

- First, awareness of how one feels physically is necessary for effective self-care.

- Second, body awareness increases emotional intelligence because emotions often register as physical sensations in the body.

- Body scan meditation is accessible and deeply relaxing even to those who are new to mindfulness.

- Potential benefits of body scan practice include increased awareness of the physical signs of stress, improved comprehension of emotions, improved ability to care for bodily needs, and enhanced ability to relax/remain calm.

Have you ever felt bad, but you couldn't say why? You might tell your spouse or text your friend and say, "I feel weird. Not sure what's up." I used to live most of my life that way. I would walk around feeling like I could cry at any moment. As a litigation associate, I was trained to push uncomfortable feelings aside, including headaches, fatigue, and even hunger. It was no big deal to ignore stress, too, until the times when I got agitated or lost my cool and couldn't ignore it anymore.

It wasn't until I started meditating that I understood what this "almost might cry" feeling was: stress. I realized that I had been feeling the effects of chronic stress—the feeling of never getting rest and always fighting some battle. How did I realize this? Because when I started to meditate, I learned how to relax, and the feeling faded away. Eventually, it disappeared, and I developed a baseline for how my neutral state felt.

Establishing the ability to stop with breath practice is important, but a body scan is also essential because it will help you understand how your body feels.

Body scan can help you continue cultivating mindfulness— the ability to focus and stay with an experience—and offer the added benefits of building comfort with and understanding of the sensations in your body. This can put you in a better position to proactively take care of your body so you can put yourself in the best position to handle the hard parts of life.

Now, you may wonder why meditation is necessary for this realization. Barring neurological damage, we all should be able to notice sensations in our bodies, right? This is true and is, in fact, why the body scan meditation you'll explore next is even possible. It is necessary for many of us, however, because lawyers are rarely in situations where we can focus just on our bodies.

Have you ever had a hangry attack? That's a situation where you feel so hungry that you become angry. Most of the time, those situations for lawyers don't happen because we lack access to food. Instead, they happen because we can't or don't want to stop a deposition or a meeting to eat.

Body scan meditation is important for lawyers because you may have trained yourself into a habit of ignoring how your body feels until it becomes too much.

Subtler sensations, like emotions, can be even easier to ignore. While things such as sadness or anger may be easy to recognize, other emotions like shame, loneliness, or guilt can be harder to identify. They may come in waves. They may be highly contextual. These emotions are some of the most powerful and damaging to our mental health, but they often go unrecognized, in part because they are so easily overshadowed by present-moment stressors. Perhaps it is also that we do not wish to recognize these emotions.

Despite the fact that lawyers spend most working hours with other people, studies reveal that we are the loneliest profession in the United States. Why? From experience, I know that part of the problem is that loneliness is hard to acknowledge. Relationships matter to law practice, so it was hard for me to accept that I was lonely because I wanted to think of myself as well-connected and part of a strong team.

Have you ever experienced something like this? Well, it's not your fault. Most of us never learn to directly experience our emotions or other sensations in our bodies.

When I started meditating, though, the stillness let the truth come out. I started to feel a lack in the pit of my belly or a sense of boredom on weekends when I didn't have big plans. One hard day, I felt a sense of deep sadness and longing. This pushed me to examine how I'd been living my life. It was hard, but I realized I had been focusing my energy on billing hours and starting my family instead of building my community.

This helped me cut through the shame that had caused me to ignore my loneliness for years and begin to change my conduct. I joined a moms group, got active in the bar association, and started accepting any invitation I got to grab lunch, go to parties, or get drinks after work. And you know what? I found out that I was good at being a friend and good at networking. I became happier, took on leadership roles in bar organizations, and my law practice thrived.

This story shows how life-changing it can be to learn to listen to your body and understand what it is telling you. In just a few minutes a day, body scan meditation can help you do that.

Though actions are essential to changing your life, your conduct often can't change unless you understand what your body is saying. This is why reconnecting with your body is essential to the cultivation of mindfulness and compassion.

In addition, since compassion is presence with suffering plus the willingness to help, it is essential to learn how to be present with the bodily sensations and emotions that inevitably arise when difficulty happens. By the end of the chapter, you will understand how critical body awareness is to letting compassion flow and the practices that can help you foster it.

BODY SCAN MEDITATION

The best way to understand body awareness is to experience it directly. One of the simplest and most common ways of doing this is the body scan meditation technique. With this practice, you focus on the sensations in your body in a systematic way rather than exclusively focusing on the breath. Generally, body scan meditations start at the crown of the head and proceed down to other parts of the body systematically.

A typical body scan meditation may go as follows: Find a comfortable and stable position where you can breathe easily and relax but also feel alert enough that you aren't likely to fall asleep. Root into your position and feel a sense of connection with the floor or your seat. Allow your spine to elongate, but don't strain. Take a full breath in, and on the exhale, allow your eyes to lower or close. Bring your attention to the very top of your head and notice whatever sensations are there. It may be tingling or feel the subtle motion of the air in the room. Just notice it, and then let that sensation melt down into:

- the back of your head, forehead, and sides of your head
- your eyes and brow
- your nose, cheeks, mouth, and chin

As you go, just feel what is there, and don't worry if it is right or wrong. Simply notice it.

Continue on, feeling the sensations of the following areas and releasing tension as you go:

- your jaw, neck, and shoulders
- your upper back and upper torso
- your mid-chest and back
- your low back and belly

Backtrack just a little back to the top of your arms and feel the sensations in your biceps and triceps, then let the awareness of sensation flow into

- your lower arms
- your hands
- the back of your palms
- the front of your palm
- each finger distinctly—thumb, pointer, middle, ring, and pinkie

Let your attention progress down into your hips and let them relax fully into your seat. After settling there for a moment, shift your attention into

- your groin, pubic region, and glutes
- your upper legs, feeling all the way around and into your hamstrings and quadriceps areas
- your knees, calves, shins, and ankles
- your feet and toes

Before you conclude, see if you can bring attention to every part of your body all at once as if you are in a bubble of sensation. Sit here for a moment and rest in this experience. When you are ready, take a full breath in and hold it for a moment. Let it go with an audible sigh, and open your eyes when you are ready.

LIKELY BENEFITS OF BODY SCAN PRACTICE

Body scan tends to be more accessible to new meditators than breath practice, but that doesn't mean it will be easy. Body scan meditation still is a focus practice, and much like breath practice, it trains the mind to stay with the physical sensations of the body. There may be times when you struggle with a body scan, just like any other practice, but as always, the benefits are likely to show up in your life first.

Here are some benefits you may experience from body scan meditation:

- awareness of your physical signs of stress
- increased ability to relax the body more quickly or more deeply
- enhanced ability to remain present for/aware of bodily sensations, including uncomfortable ones
- reduction in the physical signs of stress, including during or after your meditation practice
- increased ability to settle and stay grounded during stressful situations
- heightened awareness of what the body needs/how to care for yourself

WHY BODY SCAN MEDITATION IS AWESOME FOR LAWYERS

The object of body scan meditation is to feel the sensations in the body and notice what you feel rather than to think about the body. If it's not immediately apparent, this is important for most humans and especially lawyers because your mind won't naturally do this. Our lives are busy, and we have many distractions. The rise of technology has worsened and hastened this situation as well, which means that it wouldn't be a surprising thing for a lawyer to go an entire day without really noticing how their body feels. The result is that you can end up living life a little distanced from your body, as James Joyce describes in *Dubliners*.

As the list of benefits above demonstrates, you can change this habit with practice. The other really good news is that body scan practices are often regarded as deeply relaxing and more accessible to many new meditators. So, in the process of changing the way that you relate to your body and the world, the practice itself may feel awesome.

Body scan meditation is incredibly important because it prepares you to handle difficult experiences in life and to be present for the good ones.

With body scan meditation, you are practicing staying with the physical sensations of the body, which practices the art of staying with an experience, just like the breath practice I introduced in Chapter 4. At the same time, a body scan allows you to experience and explore other physical sensations in the body. First, it may help you notice feelings of discomfort (or comfort/joy/love, etc.) and practice not reacting immediately to them. Instead, you can learn how to be with or care for them. Second, and perhaps more importantly, it will help you understand emotions and see the connection between mind and body more clearly.

People put special significance on emotions, but when you repeatedly watch them play out, you are likely to learn a basic truth: They are physical sensations in the body. In your daily life, emotions are often influenced and perpetuated by thoughts, so you may not always see this. Because body scan practice has you focus solely on how the body feels, you can distill the sensations from your thoughts.

When you can do this, you can learn to get curious about what your bodily sensations are telling you, and it may empower you to change your life in meaningful ways.

As discussed above, body awareness matters because it can help you learn to tolerate physical sensations in the body and practice curiosity instead of judgment. Over time, this can develop into wisdom because you will learn whether the sensations comprising your emotional reactions need to play out or whether they are telling you something meaningful.

Given how stressful your job as an attorney is, this is incredibly important. Most of us lawyers are trained in law school that our feelings about a legal issue don't matter because the issue is what the law says and how we can make it work for our clients. Yet, as a practical matter, anyone who has practiced law for even a few days knows that emotions affect our cases.

Emotions affect how jurors process the facts in a trial, judges and mediators relate to parties, and how clients respond to our guidance and their relationship with the opposing party. Though we don't want to admit it, they affect how we evaluate a case and decide on the next step.

What I am telling you here isn't that your emotions *should* be driving the bus. But, without an understanding of your body and emotions, they probably already are.

Body scan meditation helps because it can foster awareness of how your body feels and how your emotions register so that you don't let them unconsciously dictate your actions. I know you may be thinking that you would never do this because you are a trained and skilled lawyer who knows how to control yourself.

When I am talking about emotions unconsciously controlling your actions, I am not making an accusation or criticism. Instead, I'm talking about basic human stuff. Let's go back to the stress response to threats again. Remember, when there is a real or perceived threat, our bodies and minds react automatically and can push us quickly into fight, flight, or freeze mode.

The object here is survival, even if real survival is not in jeopardy. This process does not just make you reactionary; it affects the overall processing of the brain. It diminishes the role of the prefrontal cortex (where your higher-level functioning and better angels reside) and, through the process of thalamic gating, can even prevent you from perceiving sensory information that doesn't relate to the threat.

So, even if you are a super lawyer, and you have the badge from Thomson Reuters to prove it, you are still a human. Because you are a human, your emotions and bodily experience will inherently affect your thinking and actions in the world. This is even more likely when you are routinely dealing with stressful situations as lawyers do.

In this way, the adage "If you can't beat them, join them" applies. You can't outsmart your emotions, and even if you want to, you can't make them go away. You can, on the other hand, make friends with your emotions and your bodily experiences, and body scan meditation is a simple, accessible, and often pleasurable way of practicing this.

- What Do You Think?

In this chapter, you learned some of the reasons why body awareness is important, but now it's time to think about why it matters to you. Consider for a moment how aware of the direct sensations in your body you are. You don't need to concern yourself with comparisons to others or try to rate how normal your situation might be. Instead, scan through your memories to get a sense of how much of your day is devoted to noticing how you feel physically. If you have regular practices, including meditation, yoga, physical exercise, or other self-care, consider how often you find yourself remaining present for the experience.

- Next Steps

Last week, you worked on the goal of meditating for five minutes. This week, we will increase that goal to ten minutes (less than 0.2 hours). Just like last week, you can add a minute or two each day until you are able to sit for ten minutes. This week, though, you will have options for your practice. You can start with a breath practice and then follow with a body scan, or try a body scan to settle and finish with a breath practice. Either way, the focus this week will be on paying closer attention to physical sensations in the body and learning to use those sensations as a tool to return attention to the present moment.

For additional resources about body awareness and more body scan meditations, subscribe to the blog at www.brilliantlegalmind.com.

What are your thoughts or insights?

CHAPTER 6

STEP 3:
CONSCIOUSLY RECONNECTING
WITH KINDNESS
(BECAUSE IT'S POWERFUL)

Chapter Summary:

- Lawyers know what kindness means, and we have all experienced it.

- Many of us have never explored how most positive emotions feel in the body.

- To cultivate compassion, it makes sense to reconnect with kindness in an intentional way by purposefully opening to and exploring positive emotional experiences.

- When we do that, we can cultivate a kinder and more generous inner response to the difficult situations we encounter in life and law practice.

- Potential benefits of joy practice include an ability to elicit positive emotions, an increased ability to experience positive emotions in daily life, a better understanding of the causes of happiness, and an improved outlook and mood.

I f you are starting a meditation practice, the odds are that you are looking for a happier life. So far, though, I haven't said much about happiness, at least not directly. We've talked about mindfulness and body awareness, which research tells us leads to happiness through more calm, better choices, and more wisdom in dealing with our personal needs and emotions. But we're lawyers, and we're always looking for a more efficient way. Is there a fast track to happiness?

Sorry, guys, but I'm going to give you a lawyer answer here and say: It depends. In truth, meditation shows you that, yes indeed, you can cut through many layers of crap that get in the way of happiness quickly. For most of us, though, habits are layered on top of each other, and personal blocks can require more time and practice to get through.

The good news is that one of the fast tracks to more happiness is being present for the joy in your life as it is.

More good news: That's the focus of this chapter, and it's simpler than you may think. Undoubtedly, you have bright spots in your life, including people who love you, things you enjoy, and the beauty of nature all around you. The problem is that life makes it easy for you to become confused about and disconnected from all of these things.

WHY LAWYERS MAY NEED TO CONSCIOUSLY RECONNECT WITH POSITIVE EMOTIONS

You are probably familiar with the study of the rhesus monkey that preferred the stuffed animal in its cage to the food and water. That study is most often cited as proof that care and comfort are needs—not mere desires—for mammals (including humans). Despite this, many lawyers still have an uncomfortable relationship with kindness. Though people say that it "pays to be kind," they also say "nice guys finish last." Lawyers don't want to finish last and so we may look for feelings of comfort from winning cases and achieving results for clients rather than tapping into it directly.

While this might be motivating in some ways, it can have dark consequences. One problem with this approach is that even lawyers at the top of their game cannot always control the results in our cases. Another problem is that seeking positive feelings through achievement may cause you to associate your worth with the results you produce. In the process, you may struggle to set personal boundaries, fail to honor your needs, emotions, and pain, and fear showing who you really are to clients, colleagues, and judges.

If you aren't careful, your situation can become like another rhesus monkey study that may be less well-known: the monster mom study. In this study, researchers repeated what they'd done before but changed the mother to make scary sounds and randomly blast the baby with cold water. Heartbreakingly, the baby still clung to the monster mommy.

What does this study matter? Clearly, it tells us that mammals desperately need comfort, but we can get confused and cling to things that seem comforting even when they hurt us.

Before you start to think I am telling you that you are no better than a scared rhesus monkey, I'm saying something altogether different. I'm saying that even the best humans may not be able to help being confused from time to time about what real kindness, comfort, and care look like. In fact, even the Buddha struggled with this.

According to the myth, the Buddha acted like the rhesus monkey seeking comfort where it could not be found before he attained enlightenment. The Buddha was a prince whose dad heard a prophecy that his son would grow up to be either a great king or a spiritual leader. King dad tried to keep his son royally inclined by making his life nothing but pleasant, but the Buddha grew disillusioned when he saw people get sick, age, and die. He left his royal life behind and, like any rebellious son, promptly overcorrected to try to find the real meaning of life.

His last attempts at wisdom included asceticism so strict that he starved and mistreated himself. One day, he recognized that this was not conducive at all to spiritual growth, and he asked a kind lady to give him rice and milk. She did, he ate, replenished some strength, and *then* the Buddha attained enlightenment.

HOW TO GET CLEAR ABOUT KINDNESS

If, like me, you are a lawyer who has ever pushed through a mediation without lunch, missed a family event because you had to finish a brief, or skipped sleep for work, you know how this story applies to you. Our jobs require us to defer gratification on basic human needs frequently, and this can become a habit that causes us to forget that we too need comfort.

I didn't notice this in myself until my first meditation retreat. I struggled because I physically hurt from sitting for hours a day instead of my usual twenty minutes. I couldn't focus because I could only feel pain. My perfectionist lawyer brain would not let me take a session off until I started obsessing about leaving. Eventually, disgusted with myself, I took a session off to stretch and take a shower. Luckily, it did the trick, and I was not only able to focus but also had an insight that I will never forget: Take care of the body first and then the mind will settle.

In retrospect, this seems basic. Clearly, when we hurt, most of us know that care or healing is needed. But how many times have you pushed personal pain aside to pursue a goal or do what you perceive to be your job? How many times have you refused to ask for help because you were concerned about how it might be perceived? Sometimes this may be the right call, but if that is too often our choice, it can teach us the lesson that our feelings don't matter.

So, what's the answer? The answer is to retrain ourselves about what real kindness feels like.

The rhesus monkey chose the monster mom in the absence of other options. What if the monkey had a real mom and the monster mom to choose from and the time to experience the difference? I'm not sure if such a study exists, but I would hope that experience might teach the monkey which one provided what it really needed.

People can do this study for themselves by going back to the basics. This is another profound lesson from the myth of the Buddha. After he got a snack and started meditating under the tree, the Buddha didn't jump to enlightenment. A demon presence called Mara visited and taunted him like Jesus experienced before he delivered the Sermon on the Mount.

The Buddha didn't fight Mara or banish him with magic but simply touched the earth, remembering that his connection to the world was his strength. He then acknowledged Mara and let him be there, robbing the spirit of power, and he went on to find enlightenment.

In the same way, Mara and monster moms can visit lawyers in many ways. Billable hour expectations can suggest that you can only feel safe if you exceed number goals each month. Aggressive tactics in litigation can tell you that you can only protect yourself by responding in kind. Client and firm expectations can suggest that you are only useful to your tribe if you secure victories, close deals, or develop new business.

But, if you touch down, you can learn that you don't only have to seek feelings of safety, protection, and connection externally. So, how do you touch down when it comes to something as basic as kindness?

Reconnecting with Real Kindness

I have told you that compassion is presence with suffering plus the willingness to help, but compassion is different from empathy in a critical respect. While empathy usually means that we are taking on the experience of another, compassion is broad enough to include ourselves. Knowing this and the fact that many lawyers may themselves be experiencing the pain of stress, if not worse, my advice is not to jump headlong into the deep end of the emotional pool.

Instead, why not do this the easy way by first reconnecting with your positive emotions?

If you want to bring more kindness to the world, doesn't it make sense to have a firm grasp on what that means? Though you may know the definition of the term, it is possible that many of us lawyers haven't connected with kindness in the experiential sense recently.

The first step, therefore, is to become more conscious of your positive emotional experiences. You have learned about basic presence and body awareness in previous chapters, so you now have the foundation needed to do this. To advance these skills towards greater compassion, however, you need to start using them to experience positive emotions directly. To do that, explore the joy practice that follows.

Joy Meditation

Joy is a wonderful emotion, but it is easy to overlook when your life is busy. It's also powerful and can be uncomfortable at times. In this practice, you will get familiar with joy with the aim of understanding it better and nourishing yourself. To that end, take a moment to do a brief joy practice. Find a comfortable and stable position and allow your back to stretch out, your shoulders and jaw to relax, and close or lower your eyes if that helps you feel more at ease.

Take a few moments to focus on your breath and fill your lungs fully with air. Then scan through your body to identify and relax any areas of tension from head to toe. If it helps you, allow your lips to curve into a smile and rest in the feelings of peace that emerge. Next, bring a situation to mind where you remember feeling joy. It can be a small moment or a big one. The details are not important; only the clear memory of joy matters.

If you can't think of a real memory, let your imagination create a scene that would make you feel joyful, perhaps good news for you or a loved one or just experiencing your dream day. Let the scene fill your mind, and as it does, notice the areas of your heart and your belly. Notice how your face and body feel. Notice how your mind feels.

Take a moment to simply linger in these sensations. Then let the scene go and check in again to notice how you feel after doing the practice. This is joy. Now that you know what it feels like, you may be in a better position to recognize it in your life and help others find it. Take a final deep breath in and out, and when you are ready, open your eyes.

Common Benefits of Joy Practice

The point of a joy practice is to reconnect with positive emotions in a direct way. The practice itself may therefore create direct benefits because it will probably feel good. Your body may feel relaxed. Your mind may be more at ease because you just reminded yourself about the really important things in life. Your heart may feel open and at ease.

Other important benefits that may emerge from this practice include:

- recognizing the difference between joy and excitement
- an ability to elicit or draw on joy in unexpected situations, including difficult times
- noticing that joy can arise in simple or seemingly insignificant situations
- better understanding of what produces a joy response for you
- increased awareness of what may create positive emotions for others
- improved confidence in your ability to find happiness and stability.

GREETING HARDSHIP WITH KINDNESS

As the above list demonstrates, doing joy practice can help you understand positive emotions better, including kindness. With time and practice, this can empower you to greet hardship with kindness. As I already explained, this is not at all what your brain wants to do.

When you read the story of the Buddha above, you may have expected him to pull out a sword and cut Mara down. The miracle of that story is that the Buddha didn't do that, and instead, as many teachers describe, he "invited Mara to tea." Now, you may be thinking, *I am a lawyer, and everything in me tells me to minimize risk. How on earth can I welcome threats in my life?*

I'm not telling you that you cannot take reasonable measures to prevent threats, but if you can first respond with a basic level of kindness and acceptance, you will, in most cases, do a better job at managing the threat.

This is challenging for most of us to do, which is why practicing it in meditation helps. One of the simplest ways to practice responding to difficulty with kindness is to do it in your meditation practice.

When your mind wanders from the breath, you may start to mentally berate yourself or physically tense up. Just notice what's going on and hold it in kindness. Later, in real life, this practice will make it easier to catch yourself starting to rush or responding to other people with aggression or anger or judging yourself for a mistake.

But how will meditating on joy help you do this? It will help because the contrast in experience will make it clearer to you when you are experiencing stress or agitation. It will also help because it will allow you a chance to rest in a peaceful and happy state and heal from the stressful and difficult aspects of your life, which will create overall stability.

In other words, joy practice is so powerful because it practices all the same skills you need to deal with difficulty: presence with and awareness of emotions.

Judgment can come in many forms. For example, if you get agitated during meditation, you may judge yourself for not being calm. If you start whining or saying something nasty to someone else during a difficult time, you may judge yourself for acting "like a child" or "being mean."

While the judgment is normal, and you don't want to treat other people or yourself badly, it isn't helpful because it takes your attention further away from the present. It also can suggest the nefarious idea that you are bad in some way, and it is hopeless to try to be better. Therefore, the better route is to stay with the negative emotion, let the judgment come and go, and respond to yourself with kindness.

DEVELOPING A KIND INNER VOICE

How do you respond with kindness? That requires you to look at your inner voice. When I first started meditating, it was shocking how nasty my inner voice was. I could not do anything right, and, it seemed, neither could anyone else.

When I did anything less than perfect, the inner voice would point it out and kick me while I was down. And when a situation was less than ideal, my inner voice would complain. This made every aspect of my life harder because I never got a rest, and it came with me into every situation, even the ones that were already risky and scary.

To change this, it is not necessary to take on affectations and aphorisms that are not natural to you. You don't have to adopt an inner kindergarten teacher voice or force yourself to respond internally to stressful situations like Snow White. Instead, you only need to tap into the basic kindness that you already have and apply it to yourself.

Doing joy practice will help you experience something fundamental: You already know very well what kindness is, what comfort is, and what is soothing.

In other words, you may quickly see that you know how to comfort others, show kindness to others, and soothe others. You may also understand more clearly what ingredients need to be present for you to experience joy and kindness yourself. With this knowledge and your life experience, you will likely see that you know exactly how to respond to difficulty with kindness. In fact, you probably do it every day for clients, colleagues, and loved ones without even thinking about it.

You can do this for yourself by reflecting on what you do procedurally to calm, soothe, and comfort others. How does your voice sound? How are your posture and approach? What do you do with your body or hands? What words do you use? How do you show that you are listening and care? Once you understand these key pieces, you can apply the same strategies to yourself in times of stress. If this is difficult, another option is to draw inspiration from the examples of supportive relatives, mentors, teachers, or coaches who helped you in times of difficulty.

Even if this feels uncomfortable at first, this new approach can have life-changing results.

Deeply ingrained habits don't change overnight. Watching this change unfold is part of the essential learning that may help the change last because you will slowly experience the difference between responding to your struggles with harshness versus kindness.

It is the difference between beating yourself up all weekend because the court rejected a critical motion and reminding yourself that you did your best and asking a loved one for support. It is the difference between ignoring how scared you are about a case and wasting energy resisting it and admitting the fear and learning to coach yourself through it.

The really good news is that you don't have to do this every time. After you do it a few times, you learn that you have a choice to bring kindness and comfort into your life and law practice whenever you need it.

Ultimately, lawyers are not that different from the rhesus monkey looking for a soft place to rest or the Buddha. Though comfort is essential to your survival, and this need has the potential to lead you astray, when coupled with mindfulness, it can also guide you back to goodness and yourself. Like every other human on the planet, the capacity for joy and kindness is wired into you. To find true comfort in your life that you can share in your law practice, the first place to look is within yourself.

- What Do You Think?

Take a moment to consider what this chapter means for you. Do you accept that kindness is a human need, or are you unsure? Either way, take a moment to consider this for yourself and journal about the reasons for either answer. If you think kindness is essential, identify why you think so and any experiences that you have had that are foundational to this understanding. If you are less sure, write down your concerns without judging yourself or your past experiences.

Next, consider whether you have ever had experiences where you looked for kindness, comfort, or positive emotions in the wrong place. Did you stay in a relationship or a job too long that didn't serve you? Did you develop any habits intended to help you feel better but that you later realized made you feel worse? Again, without judging yourself for pursuing what any human being would, consider and write down your experiences and think about what you learned from those experiences.

- Next Steps

You have done so well over the last two weeks, so keep it up. This week, you will again work to add five more minutes to your meditations for a total of fifteen minutes (less than 0.3 hours). My recommendation for the style is to use a body scan to settle, then transition to a breath-focus practice for the middle of the practice, and conclude with a joy practice.

If you have trouble chunking your practice in this way, some meditation apps or other timers have functions to chime at regular intervals, or you could do a series of five-minute practices with a pause in between. You can select a new joyful memory each day or return to the same one multiple times to see if anything new comes up for you. The goal this week is to notice what happens in the mind and body as you tolerate sitting for longer periods of time and consciously reflect on joy.

To understand more about how to cultivate presence with positive emotions in your life and law practice, subscribe to the blog at www.brilliantlegalmind.com.

What are your thoughts or insights?

Chapter 7
PUTTING THE PIECES TOGETHER

Chapter Summary:

- Research shows that loving-kindness practice can increase happiness, reduce rumination, and improve relationships.
- It is a dynamic combination of the three things we learned in the preceding chapters.
- In this style of practice, you not only experience positive emotions but also cultivate them by bringing people or groups to mind and wishing them well.
- This practice may feel uncomfortable or even produce negative responses at first, but with time, it can help you learn about yourself and build emotional stability.

Now that you have learned the fundamentals, it is time to put them together so they can work for you in life. Before you do this, it may help to remember your intention. You are probably reading this book to look for a new way of dealing with the stress and hardships of law practice and life, right? In Chapter 1, you learned that mindfulness and compassion could help you stay present with difficulty and remain willing to help. You also discovered how this ability to bring kindness to difficulty could protect you from the harmful effects of stress, even as it helped you make wiser decisions.

In the previous three chapters, you explored the fundamentals so that you could more effectively combine mindfulness, body awareness, and positive emotions to let compassion flow when needed. In this chapter, you'll put all of those skills together and practice offering kindness to yourself and the world.

The result of doing this practice over time is that you will more likely respond to life situations with compassion, which means more presence, less judgment, and less stress.

The ingredients you learned in Chapters 4 to 6 work together in the practice you will explore here: loving-kindness, or metta, as it is traditionally called. Some people struggle with loving-kindness practice at first, but it has been my favorite style of meditation for many years. I tend to be judgmental and rational, so I spent much of my life in cave number one from Chapter 2. When I tried loving-kindness practice, I got to experience what cave number two felt like, and it was exactly what I needed.

The truth is, I didn't start and continue with loving-kindness practice to become a saint. Instead, I did it for self-preservation. One of the first times I did the practice was after one of the worst depositions I ever took. The witness spent more time playing games than answering questions, and opposing counsel blatantly attempted to bully and confuse me. I left the first day feeling like a failure because the witness's story was still unclear and frustrated because I had another day to go.

I came home, vented to my husband, and then did loving-kindness practice. It was like wrapping myself in a warm blanket. It reminded me that all people (and even all lawyers) are not terrible and that I was not alone. I went to the deposition the next day and finished up.

When I saw the witness play the same games with the other defense counsel, I realized I wasn't the problem at all. Because I had cared for my feelings the night before, I was able to see it. When it came time for summary judgment, I channeled my frustration for opposing counsel into an excellent brief, and we ultimately got a good result on the case as a whole.

In other words, loving-kindness practice can help you manage the judgment and reactivity that comes with law practice. It also feels really good, so it can become a new form of self-care.

As you will see below, loving-kindness practice is about wishing yourself and others well. Now, you may be worried that wishing in itself is not enough to create real change. That is true, but loving-kindness practice is not merely wishing. Instead, it is about connecting with your heart and expanding your mind to cultivate kindness so you can bring it more reliably into your life and law practices. By practicing sending kindness outward, you are priming yourself to respond to yourself, others, and difficult life situations with kindness. Over time, that cultivates compassion.

THE PRACTICE METHOD

1. Take a few moments or minutes to find a relaxed but alert posture and settle the mind. A breath practice or body scan can help you do this.

2. Bring attention to the area of your heart. Focus on the sensations in your heart as you call people to mind and wish them the phrases below. You focus on this area because it is where positive emotions tend to register. You may not notice anything at first, and that's okay. However, possible sensations to look for include a sense of warmth, fullness, or even expansion in the heart area.

3. Bring the person or group to mind and offer phrases of loving-kindness to each one. Notice sensations in your body and thoughts or emotions that arise as you do.

4. This practice is about cultivating loving-kindness and compassion for yourself and others, so don't judge yourself if you don't feel much. In addition, don't judge yourself if anger, resentment, or other feelings come up instead. Those may help you acknowledge your feelings and address issues in a skillful way. Let whatever comes up arise and give yourself time. The patience you show yourself is likely to translate to how you treat others.

5. Continue with other individuals/groups until you reach the end of the sequence or your meditation time.

6. Allow yourself a few moments to return to neutral after the practice is over because the practice can be emotional. Return to the breath or a body scan or simply sit before ending the meditation and moving on to another activity.

THE PHRASES OF LOVING-KINDNESS

The traditional phrases for loving-kindness practice are as follows:

- May I/you/we be happy
- May I/you/we be healthy
- May I/you/we be safe
- May I/you/we be at peace (or at ease)

These phrases are as simple as "have a nice day," but they mean more because they go directly to our most fundamental human needs. Having been raised Catholic, their formal language never bothered me. The number of times I have said "may peace be with you" while shaking hands in church are so numerous that I automatically think *and also with you* when I see memes saying, "May the force be with you."

If these phrases make you feel like you are doing an impersonation of Obi-Wan Kenobi, that's no problem. You could keep practicing for a while to see if it starts to feel more natural. As I discussed in the last chapter, this practice may represent an identity shift, so it is normal to feel awkward. Watching those reactions come and go benefits you if you can hold them tenderly instead of becoming reactive.

Another option is to change the phrases. One great thing about loving-kindness practice is that it is flexible. In Buddhism, loving-kindness (or essential friendliness) is only one of the four brahma viharas (heart practices). The other three are: caruna (compassion), mudita (sympathetic joy), and upekkha (equanimity).

As a result, many teachers use the format of loving-kindness or metta practice but change the phrases to work on these other three traits. As such, you can feel free to tailor the phrases to suit your needs. If you want to do this,

you can go to http://brilliantlegalmind.com/resources/
the-heart-of-loving-kindness-practice-guide-2/ to download
a guide to help you craft your own phrases.

THE PEOPLE

When you start with loving-kindness practice, the general
recommendation (and one that I subscribe to) is to start
slow. If you are called on to think of a loved one, start with
someone easy to love with little baggage. Conversely, when
you are called on to think of a difficult person, think of
someone who merely annoyed or confused you recently and
not your mortal enemy.

This practice is about cultivating kindness, so the first step
is not pushing yourself too hard too fast and trusting in your
ability to grow over time. The following is the traditional list
of people who are the focal points of loving-kindness practice,
but you can change the order or do only portions of this list
in different combinations depending on time constraints or
preference.

SELF

The first focal point for loving-kindness practice, yourself,
may be the hardest. Many people struggle with this aspect of
the practice though the reasons can vary. Some struggle with
grammar and wonder how they can simultaneously be the
offeror and recipient of well wishes. In that case, modify the
language and instead envision it as the universe or a higher
power sending you safety, peace, happiness, and health. In
this scenario, all you must do is receive the wishes as they
rain down.

Some find it uncomfortable to overtly send love to themselves. If this is the struggle, you can start by thinking of the

loved one or mentor first and then returning to yourself when the heart is opened. Another option is to think of yourself at a different time in your life. Thinking of a past version of yourself can help you not worry about the logical realities, and seeing yourself as a child may evoke tender feelings.

LOVED ONE

The loved one can be anyone who is easy for you to love, including friends, relatives, or even pets. Choose someone who is not complicated for you. The loved one should be someone easy to love because they are someone who can help you open your heart and reconnect with positive emotions. Thus, the test I use to determine if someone counts as a loved one is this: It should be someone who would cause you automatically to smile and walk towards them for a big handshake or hug (or a lick or belly rub if it's a pet) if you hadn't seen them for a while.

MENTOR

Mentors are important to law practice, but in loving-kindness practice, this person does not have to be a mentor in the professional sense. Instead, I view the mentor in the sense of that term as used in Joseph Campbell's hero's journey. The mentor could be anyone you found along the journey of your life who helped you, supported you, gave you a gift, or taught you something. Parents, teachers, coaches, doctors, therapists, spiritual leaders, or wise friends often fit this bill. The role of the mentor in loving-kindness practice is to continue opening our hearts and remind us of our deep connections to others and the power of all humans to help each other. It also reminds us that even powerful, wise, and supportive people need support, love, and kindness.

NEUTRAL

The neutral person in loving-kindness meditation is one that I have found to be the most surprising. This is a person in your life whom you know enough to recognize their face, but you may not know their name or other information about them. This could be your barista at Starbucks, your mail carrier or Amazon delivery person, a person in your office who isn't in your practice group, or that neighbor you have seen but never had a chance to meet. This part of the practice expands the concept of kindness to include strangers.

Imagination is required because the details of the person's life are unknown, but this is what engenders transformation. It reminds us that all humans want to be safe, healthy, happy, and at peace and have their own hopes, dreams, fears, and struggles. Because lawyers deal with a variety of people in our work, it is an excellent practice to help us see the opportunities for kindness in our everyday lives.

DIFFICULT

The words "difficult person" may evoke thoughts of opposing counsel that you cannot stand. This is normal, but I suggest that you don't rush there at the beginning. Don't pick your biggest opponent or the person who wronged you most recently first. Instead, select someone less challenging. Remember, in all things, the practice is self-kindness. Don't start a new practice with the hardest thing first. Instead, work up to them by working with people who annoyed or confused you recently. After a while, you may be ready to use difficult opposing counsel in loving-kindness practice, and you may be surprised to see the impact it can have.

Note: The difficult person can be your loved one. In fact, a loved one may be a great difficult person to choose if the hurt they caused is not so great or deep that it will derail your practice. This part of the practice is where your heart stretches, so this may be where you could experience more difficulty. If judgment or other negative emotions arise, that's normal. If possible, avoid judging yourself for being human, notice what comes up, and use your breath or body to restabilize if needed.

COMMUNITY AND THE WORLD

The final part of the practice is where you transition from sending loving-kindness from individuals to groups. The normal progression is to start with your household or family, then your community, your nation or region, the whole world, and finally, all living things. This is like the practice for the neutral person but with a slow and dramatic zoom-out effect to cover all of creation.

I find that, by the time I have finished practicing with the individuals, I can let my mind and heart broaden to send love out to the world at large. How you visualize this part of the practice is up to you, but it is essential to understand the connection between kindness and the state of your community and the world. In other words, this part of the practice is the bridge between your wishes of kindness and action out in the real world.

WHAT IF I DON'T FEEL LOVING-KINDNESS RIGHT AWAY?

The goal (and I use that term loosely) of loving-kindness practice is to cultivate comfort with the sensations of positive emotions in your heart. Regardless, these feelings may not emerge right away or occur in every session. If you are new to meditation, it may be hard to feel any sensations in the heart area at first. It took time before I was still enough to sense my heart beating when I meditated, even though it was certainly doing so. The absence of warm, loving sensations right away may cause those new to the practice to wonder if they are doing something wrong.

We all know, however, that you can't control how you feel. It's no different in loving-kindness practice. Our emotions can get mixed up very easily. Love can be tinged with sadness and doubt. Anger can mask fear or hurt, and judgment can reflect discomfort with oneself or one's lack of control. Being busy can mask them all.

When you try loving-kindness practice, it's healthy to let whatever emotions you experience breathe. Besides that, you can learn a lot by noticing the negative reactions that come out of loving-kindness practice.

The good news is that with meditation, everything is workable.

You can practice nonjudgmental awareness of the emotion and then respond to it with kindness by offering yourself the phrase, "May I forgive myself." You can also learn from the difficulty itself. It can alert you to hard feelings that perhaps you had overlooked or ignored. Though these are hard emotions to experience, holding them in kindness and giving them room to breathe can empower you off the cushion to, perhaps, be extra careful with yourself or do the necessary work to repair a relationship.

In this way, the path to cultivating feelings of loving-kindness and overall happiness is, in part, sifting through and developing kindness for all of your emotions. Much like in strength training, you won't feel strong while lifting heavy weights because the point of the exercise is to create enough tension and struggle to build strength. In the same way, loving-kindness is exercising your heart and mind in a new way and pushing you to stretch and open wider than they may have been opened before. This is not easy work, but the challenge is worth it.

- What Do You Think?

Be honest with yourself. Does it seem weird to practice kindness? If it does, don't stress. As I have discussed throughout this book, kindness is an innate trait for most of us. Thus, we can easily associate a person's kindness with their essential character. However, we also know that kindness is an act too, and it is often affected by context.

With that in mind, take a moment to think about times in your life when you had to do something challenging or scary, and you practiced to prepare for it. This could be a situation from work, such as a big client meeting or an oral argument, or from your life, like a difficult conversation with a loved one. Consider how your efforts to prepare showed kindness for yourself and the other people involved, and journal a few paragraphs about your insights.

- Next Steps

You are in the final week of the program. Congratulations! This week, the goal is to sit for twenty minutes (less than 0.4 hours). If that seems like a lot, it shows how far you have come. By now, however, you have many strategies to use. You have the breath to establish focus, you have body scanning to relax tension, and you have a joy practice to bring kindness in whenever needed.

You can use the time in meditation to settle the mind and then do a full loving-kindness practice. If that seems like too much for you right now, you can also use the same strategy from last week, starting with a body scan and breath focus and then concluding with a brief loving-kindness practice for only one or two of the people identified above each session. This may help you memorize the people in the practice and build comfort with it over time.

Loving-kindness practice is a favorite of mine, and I write about it frequently on my blog. To learn more about it and try some additional practices, subscribe at www.brilliantlegalmind.com.

What are your thoughts or insights?

PART III
REAPING THE BENEFITS OF MINDFULNESS AND COMPASSION

Chapter 8

HOW MINDFULNESS AND COMPASSION GRADUALLY TRANSFORM LIFE AS A LAWYER

- It is normal to sometimes struggle with meditation practice.
- The benefits of a meditation practice may be subtle at first and will surprise you.
- If you allow sufficient time to develop skills with practice, benefits could include fewer physical signs of stress, less rushing, more awareness of thoughts, increased self-compassion, and more concern for others.
- The measure of a meditation practice is not how any session feels but instead how your life improves overall, including the way that you respond to setbacks, challenges, and adversity.

B y now, you've had a chance to read about and even try all of the practices over the course of four weeks. Or maybe you're a skeptic like me and you haven't started yet because you want to read and understand first what you may be getting yourself into. Both responses are perfectly fine.

You've learned throughout this book about the benefits that a regular meditation practice can impart, including reduced stress, increased happiness, less rumination, and better relationships. Exactly what benefits will emerge for you and on what timetable, however, is not as clear. It may depend on the amount and type of meditation you do, your personality, and your habits of mind.

If you have tried out the practices in the last few weeks, you are likely to have encountered some struggles, including boredom, frustration, confusion, or an overwhelming amount of nasty thoughts or emotions. All of this is normal and, I would argue, ultimately beneficial. Why? Because the benefits don't happen because meditation is relaxing. The benefits come because struggles in meditation teach us to relax, focus again, and offer kindness to whatever arises.

STRUGGLES IN MEDITATION PRACTICE DON'T MEAN YOU ARE DOING IT WRONG

For most of us, the goal of meditation is to find peace, stability, focus, and calm. So, when we sit down to practice, we look for personal transformation and development. We are looking for a better way. How do humans usually find a "better way" of doing things? Most commonly, you usually beat your head against a wall until you learn a new way.

Meditation can suck when you start practicing because it feels like you are doing everything wrong. In reality, you are doing something hard. You are looking at stuff you've ignored most of your life, and you may have few skills to deal with it. You are also doing something "spiritual," which puts pressure on you to do it "right." Therefore, while mindfulness and compassion practices can help you redecorate your inner mental cave, it may take some time to build the skills to complete the renovation.

This is why it's brave to commit to the practices and keep going even when you experience difficulty and discomfort. Remember, the mind doesn't want to stay put, see things as they are, or respond to difficulty with kindness. It wants to judge it, banish it, and ignore it. By sitting to meditate, you are putting a flag in the ground of your life and embarking on a whole new conquest: understanding yourself.

SEEING REALITY IS ESSENTIAL FOR PERSONAL DEVELOPMENT

Although we say "nobody's perfect," lawyers implicitly expect ourselves to be. Because so many people depend on you, it can seem that perfection is required to serve them. Your normal habit may be to hide or overlook your imperfections. When you meditate, though, you intentionally make a choice to set all the distractions aside and look at yourself, including the imperfections. That's not only brave; it's essential to making necessary change.

You know this from your law practice. I get vague texts or emails from clients all the time asking me for my legal advice, and I almost always respond with two words: "Call me." Why? I do this because I need to understand the situation fully and a factual overview no more detailed than a bar exam question isn't enough. I don't just need to answer them; I need to give them a path forward that will put them in the best position possible. So, I need to get down in the dirt and make sense of the messy situation.

Mindfulness and compassion are the same. You are getting down in the dirt of your own messy situation because when you do that, you can find and remove blocks to innate compassion. As you know from your law practice, removing blocks can be frustrating work. At first, therefore, many aspects of meditation practice may be uncomfortable, to say the least. Facing the discomfort, slowly and gradually, is how the benefits emerge.

BENEFITS WILL LIKELY EMERGE GRADUALLY AND MAY SURPRISE YOU

As you might experience, it didn't feel good when I first started meditating. I was lost in thought, I saw how nasty my inner dialogue was, I got angry every time something disrupted me, and I had to experience physical discomfort. The thing that I liked, though, was the tiniest thing in the world. It was the experience of stopping for a moment. I was dizzy with activity as a litigation associate and new mom, so meditating felt like reaching out for a wall to find my balance. In short, it felt good to stop, even though stopping came with its own challenges.

So, I kept going. I didn't immediately get mental clarity or tame the nasty voice in my head, but I made progress on another pain point, quite literally. I used to have neck pain and headaches so bad that I saw a chiropractor.

When I meditated, I noticed little crackles as the muscles in my face, neck, and shoulders released. My unconsciously furrowed brow would flatten, and my jaw would unclench. My normally screen-strained eyes would rest, too, as I sat with my eyes closed. When the timer chimed, I almost always felt better. My energy was restored and any pain I may have had at the outset was reduced or gone.

What this means to you is that the benefits of your meditation practice may not be mental or emotional right away. Instead, physical benefits may show up first, but those benefits can affect you in many ways.

Because meditation helped me feel physically better, I stuck with it even though the mental benefits took longer to emerge. Though they were subtle at first, they came soon enough. The first thing I noticed was my tendency to rush.

On a trip to the grocery store a few weeks after I started meditating, I was storming through the aisles like a contestant on *Supermarket Sweep*. Suddenly, it occurred to me that I had no time constraints, was blessed with a few minutes by myself, and I could take my time. I immediately slowed down to stop and smell the . . . produce, and the whole experience became more enjoyable. Though I still find myself rushing at times, I am now practiced at seeing it and easing back.

One Benefit of Meditation May Be the Absence of Old Problems

If you give yourself more time practicing, more pronounced and significant changes are likely to emerge. I have struggled for most of my life with overthinking. I would worry about things that *might* happen in the future and agonize about things I *should* have done or failed to do in the past. Any challenge that came up in life prompted a complex scheme about the best course of action that was so protracted it left me exhausted and scared to act at all.

In one of the worst examples, I remember spending an entire weekend (time I could have spent with my friends or family) trying to perfect a motion for summary judgment for a client though it was clearly plagued by factual disputes. While it was my job to do my best, my efforts were inefficient and ultimately useless. The case was resolved on its own soon after, and my struggle to fix what I couldn't had been a waste.

A few months after I started meditating, though, the overthinking disappeared. It felt like magic, but in reality, meditation helped me learn something fundamental: noticing that I was thinking. Whereas before, when I thought and schemed about things, I would implicitly assume that I was in a version of reality or, at worst, having a conversation with the voice of reason.

What this means for you is that regular meditation practice may help you internalize the fact that thinking is merely thinking.

Sometimes it's useful and true, and sometimes it isn't. Meditation lets you see this because it provides a safe container to let thoughts come and go and bounce around. When you see them this way, you can see that thoughts just happen, and sometimes they are useless, silly, or plain bonkers.

After a while, you will likely be able to do this when you aren't meditating. A thought may occur to you, and instead of believing it or acting on it, you can ask yourself whether it is true.

The simple act of challenging your thoughts can free you from a lot of personal pain.

As one example, I used to worry that I was a bad mom because I do local government work and have a lot of night meetings. An unspoken rule dictated that I shouldn't be out of the house for more than two nights during the week. Of course, with meetings and networking and community events, this happened regularly, and a wave of guilt always hit me. One day, though, I saw the wave coming and asked myself,

"Wait, is it true that I have to be home three nights a week to be a good mom?"

I searched my mind to find the origins of this rule and found nothing. Then I tested it with my husband, a CPA who regularly worked late on consecutive days during tax season. I asked him if he had ever worried about how many nights he was home during the week, and he didn't just say "no." He laughed and asked, "Why?" with genuine bewilderment about how I had come up with such a question.

Stunned and maybe a little hacked off, I explained the worry that I had never shared with anyone before. He reminded me that I'm not a mom only at night or during the week and that doing my job was, in part, why I was a good one. Though I've had other mom guilt attacks since then, I've never worried about violating that so-called rule again.

ULTIMATELY MINDFULNESS AND COMPASSION BECOME SKILLS YOU CAN USE

With more time and experience, a few minutes of meditation each day can also help you face some even trickier problems as you start to better understand your emotions. When you become familiar with sensations in your body, you'll likely be proactive about managing your fatigue and emotions. I did this one day when I had twelve hours of trial prep, bar activities, and an evening board of education meeting. Knowing how this would feel by the end of the day, I packed a healthy lunch, took opportunities to take quick walks outside on breaks, and even meditated for a few minutes in the parking lot before heading into the next event. At the end of the day, I felt tired, of course, but proud for remaining attentive and productive throughout.

Awareness of bodily sensations can help you manage your heart more effectively too. I experienced this in a contentious meeting where the opposing party became frustrated and yelled at my client. When this happened, I noticed what felt like electricity running up and down my arms. I sat with it for a moment as I processed what was happening. This gave me the presence of mind to not engage the angry man and make him angrier but instead to address opposing counsel and calmly suggest a break. She readily agreed, and the meeting resumed without incident a few minutes later.

When I speak with lawyers and firms, I always present mindfulness as practical more than anything else because it can help you avoid mistakes, conflicts, and wastes of time and energy.

Now, before you start to get skeptical, there will, of course, be times when mindfulness won't save you and you'll lose your cool or fail to act as you should. The good news, though, is that mindfulness and compassion offer quicker and more reliable ways of getting back on track. When self-compassion is part of your skill set, you'll be better at apologizing and admitting when you are wrong. Like me, you'll still hate it when you have to do this because you're a lawyer who likes to be right. Even so, you may experience less deep shame and physical pain with the apology, which is a huge relief.

This seems like magic, but it's really just common sense. Among other things, meditation practices self-kindness and nonjudgment. All that time watching your mind wander and coming back without beating yourself up is practice for dealing with setbacks in life. Though this can be hard, it is all training for life as a lawyer. When mistakes happen at work, you often don't have time to fret, worry, and blame; you have to focus instead on solving the problem.

This is why the results of mindfulness and compassion training can be so powerful: They help you let go of the stuff you don't need, so you can focus even amidst stress.

For instance, I was grateful for my mindfulness practice on a day I had a position statement due that I had neglected to calendar. Instead of wasting time panicking or berating myself, I evaluated my options, spoke with my assistant to discuss a game plan, and got the project done in time to file.

In another situation, I lost my cool with a difficult witness on the first day of a lengthy hearing. I had driven three hours to get there that morning and was exasperated and exhausted by the end of the day. That night, I worried about what my client and the hearing officer might think, but I ultimately concluded that the only thing I could do was not repeat the behavior. So, I forgave myself, spent some time organizing my notes to be efficient the next day, and relaxed so I could get a good night's sleep. To my surprise, I later got a good decision and a gift from the client to thank me for my efforts.

Over time, you may notice the even more powerful result that you can coach yourself through challenges and develop greater self-confidence.

Even if, like me, you are a doubter by nature, a kind response to setbacks can change everything because you start to trust that you will have your own back. Sure, mistakes may come with consequences, but it may no longer feel like your self-worth is on the line in every challenge. As one example of this, I remember feeling nervous when I tried my first solo jury trial, but I was still able to act intuitively, improvise without handwringing, and even enjoy myself because I knew I could handle it if something went wrong.

Learning to be easier with yourself is not only necessary because law practice moves fast and mistakes are bound to happen. It can also help you respond more gently and effectively to others in your life. When you understand intimately how emotions like shame or letting others down can feel, you may find it natural to deploy compassion to assure a terrified witness for cross-examination. By doing the work to understand your emotions in meditation, you can help the people in your life and law practice manage how they feel at times when it matters most.

THE MEASURE OF A MEDITATION PRACTICE IS THE IMPACT ON YOUR LIFE

You may notice that I have never said that a perfect meditation practice is necessary for any of these benefits to emerge. I still have days that I miss practice due to my schedule, inner resistance, or laziness. There are times when I fall asleep, can't focus, or sit with negative feelings, pain, irrelevant fantasies about things that will never happen, or bad memories from the past. None of this bothers me now. Why?

As I say every time I teach meditation to lawyers, the point isn't to have a good meditation session but instead to have a good life.

Famed meditation teacher, Joseph Goldstein, agrees that this is how you measure a meditation practice, not by the experiences on the cushion, but by the life you live away from it, including whether you are happier, rushing less, more aware of how you feel, and more mindful of others' feelings. In short, the goal of meditation isn't to be good at meditation or even to feel good when you are doing it. Instead, the goal is, overall, to have a better life.

Research has revealed in so many ways that a few minutes of meditation each day can do this for us, but it can be hard to remember that when you start practicing. It can be hard to see how clarity comes from confusion, kindness can emerge from anger and judgment, or confidence is born from failure and frustration.

If you remember nothing else, though, remember that clarity comes from meditation because you've made the effort to seek understanding. Kindness emerges from meditation because you practiced staying present with failure and frustration.

That's why meditation is maddening and magical. It's why everybody doesn't do it, even though it could benefit so many. It's why you are a badass for trying it or even just thinking about it. Meditation isn't about being calm or quieting your mind. It's about seeing who you really are, whether you are calm or not, and living in the noisy, messy world. If you give yourself time with the practice and offer patience to yourself, you'll not only see who you really are but be in a better position to be who you want to be as a lawyer and a human being.

- What Do You Think?

Now that you've had a chance to read about and try the practices in this book, take a moment to consider how you are doing. Is there any aspect of meditation that you are starting to enjoy? Are any benefits starting to emerge for you? Regardless of how subtle or small they are, take a few minutes to identify them, discuss them with a friend, or write about them in your journal.

- Next Steps

Although I spent some time in this chapter explaining that meditation is often hard, this doesn't mean that it has to be a struggle forever. Eventually, meditation should start to feel a bit easier, even if hard sessions still occur due to the normal ups and downs of life. Identify or write down any pain points in your practice. Is your posture uncomfortable? Do you regularly nod off? Then consider whether you can add tools, such as a meditation cushion or app, to better support your practice. If you need help thinking about this, check out the *Pause and Begin Again* ebook on my blog for more ideas: http://brilliantlegalmind.com/resources/pause-and-begin-again-e-book/.

What are your thoughts or insights?

CHAPTER 9

TOO BUSY TO BREATHE? HOW LAWYERS CAN MAINTAIN A ~~PERFECT~~ MEDITATION PRACTICE

- Your meditation practice does not have to be perfect to have a positive impact on your life.
- Flexibility is critical for lawyers who want to make mindfulness and compassion a regular part of their lives because change happens and our lives are busy.
- The focus should be on maintaining the habit and returning to the practice without judgment, even if you miss a session or a period of practice.
- Informal mindfulness and compassion practices are healthy ways to cope with the challenges of life and law practice and useful means of maintaining the habit of mindfulness even in hectic times.

Now you've finished most of the book, and hopefully, you have been trying the practices over the last four weeks. You may be feeling a huge sense of accomplishment, but as most of us know, that feeling is often accompanied by an uncomfortable question: Now what? Over the last four weeks, you've had a clear directive to learn meditation practices and a goal to develop some skills. You were on a track, but now that track is ending.

Don't panic! It's okay. You got this.

As with any new habit, you may be having some anxiety about maintaining it. Have you ever started a new and healthy habit and felt great after a few weeks in, but you were still nervous about whether you could keep it going? We all have done that, and lawyers are bound to do this tons of times over the course of our careers. You are busy. Your life can change rapidly, and change inevitably will affect your habits.

So what's a lawyer to do if you want to keep meditating because you know it is good for you?

This question seems hard, but the truth is that it's quite simple. You just keep meditating because you know it's good for you.

Now, you may be thinking: *No, it's not at all simple for me. And, by the way, screw you.* That's fair. I am getting into semantics here. Note that I said "simple" and not "easy." I know it can be a challenge to fit meditation into a schedule and come back to it when you slip. But if you adopt the simple strategy of returning to your practice, it will still be in your life.

This approach is simple in the sense that there's just one option: Get back to it. It's also simple in the sense that you dispense with self-judgment about your discipline and handwringing about doing the practice wrong. Though these are normal and human tendencies for lawyers who literally get paid to think, they don't really matter in the long run.

The thing that really matters for keeping mindfulness and compassion in your life long-term is getting back to meditation whenever you can.

Now, maybe this sounds like crazy talk to you, but it's really no different than most of your other habits. Most of us humans have a pretty well-established habit of eating at regular intervals, but most of us have also missed or delayed a meal on occasion because of our schedules or things like illness. None of us would think *I must not be very good at eating, so I will just give up.* Why is meditation any different? It's not.

Sure, I know that meditation isn't essential to life in the same way that food is. I know that, unlike food, you can survive without meditation. But that only means you have a choice to meditate to obtain the benefits. While this choice may make it harder to make meditation a habit in your life, it also means that you can relax a bit more about so-called mistakes.

Why does this matter? It matters because you don't have to have a perfect meditation practice to benefit your life.

I know I have spent half of this book giving you a nice little pathway and a defined structure to building a meditation practice. I did so on purpose because we need structure to learn concepts, and we need steps to build skills and explore practices. In life, however, you are likely to find that your practice may be much more flexible.

I may be the only meditation teacher to say this, but a flexible approach is the ideal way to use meditation as a practicing lawyer.

After about ten years of meditation, I have settled into a practice that is relatively consistent. I do about thirty minutes every day and use a timer that chimes at ten-minute intervals so I can easily break it into thirds. In the first third, I may use some breath practice or a body scan to settle. In the middle, I just sit, and in the last third, I will usually do some form of compassion practice.

I don't use guided meditations anymore because, honestly, I got sick of having to pick one every time I meditated. Eventually, I learned that I prefer the space that silence offers. If you choose to support your practice with guided meditations, that's wonderful. There are now many excellent apps or online meditations (including on my blog) to choose from, and you can learn a lot by using them.

As your practice evolves, though, I encourage you to try some unguided meditation just in case you like it. It's also handy to have some experience meditating without guidance because you'll be prepared to guide yourself if you ever need to focus on the breath in real life. While it is ideal to eventually settle into a relatively routine practice, it's also a good idea to explore new styles and methods to learn new skills or reinvigorate your practice. In fact, this is how I developed my practice: by playing around, exploring, and testing what worked for me.

The important thing here is to stop worrying about doing meditation the "right way" so you can focus on finding what works for you.

In part, this means understanding the difference between a habit and a streak. A streak happens when you meditate day after day without interruption. Those can sometimes be fun and motivating and can help you establish or reestablish a habit. Clearly, if you can meditate every day without fail, you are a rockstar, and you may see more benefits than me or the other folks who can't.

So what? Who are you competing with here? Do you really need to be the best at meditation?

I meditate most days and sometimes get into a nice streak, but I occasionally miss days. Some days I am sick or too tired. Some days I just forget. Some days my schedule or my kids' schedules leaves me no time. Or some days I do another mindfulness practice, like yoga, and don't feel the need to meditate too.

Sure, this is not ideal if my aim is to maximize my mindfulness (whatever that means). But I don't care because I don't live in an ideal world. I live in the ordinary, imperfect world and have learned that I am much happier and better to everyone around me when I accept that I'm imperfect too.

Here's why this is important. It means you can relax and forgive yourself if you miss practice.

The benefits of mindfulness practice do not slip away after missing practice for one or even a few days. Instead, what will likely happen is that missing meditation may make you want to come back to it, much like missing a few days of exercise can make you feel uncomfortable and cranky. In my experience, missing practice causes me to rush more than usual, resist life more, or feel like I have a clog of thoughts in my brain. When I sit again, I feel better, and it reminds me why I practice at all.

As a perfectionist lawyer, I used to see things like this as a failure. Mindfulness practice, however, helps you see things as just another life experience. When you train yourself to pay attention to what's in your mind and how your body feels, those facts start to matter more than your judgments about them.

Now, this isn't to say that missing practice long-term won't have an impact. Brain plasticity is both brilliant and a burden in this regard. If you stop practicing for long enough, you are going to notice. I don't encourage you to stop practicing just to check me on this because habits can be tricky beasts. Even so, most of us lawyers are likely to experience this for ourselves at some point.

If your practice lapses for a while, the approach remains the same: Don't panic and don't judge. Pay attention and see what happens.

Though I have positioned myself as a fancy schmancy meditation teacher, I must confess that I am a mere mortal. In fact—gasp!—I, too, faced a considerable dereliction with my meditation habit. Despite the fact that I was convinced early on of the power of my practice, I stopped meditating for almost a year. I had the best of intentions of getting back to it but never did until—foolish mortal that I am—I started having problems.

Specifically, the overthinking that I thought I had gotten over came roaring back. Slowly but surely, I became obsessed with the news and worried so much about the state of the world that a family member told me I should "talk to someone." I wasn't above therapy, but I took this for the red flag it was. I started meditating regularly again to see if it helped since I knew it would take a while to get an appointment anyway.

It helped me immediately. Obviously, it didn't fix the world, but it helped me disrupt thought spirals so I could focus on what I could do to help and let go of what I couldn't control. The best thing is that I didn't just feel better; I did better. Once I had reclaimed the energy I had been spending on overthinking, I saw my community involvement had lapsed due to life changes, and I got involved with new committees and boards for causes that mattered to me.

In other words, the lapse in my practice was a life lesson for which I'm now grateful because it taught me how important and effective meditation is for me. It opened my eyes and reinvigorated my practice so much that I then started doing retreats, getting more training, and eventually writing and speaking about mindfulness.

I say this all the time when I teach mindfulness to lawyers and firms: An imperfect meditation practice with flaws and failures can still change your life in ways you could never imagine.

If you are a disciplined person who lives life on a clock-work schedule, don't disrupt it for my sake. You do you. Do what most meditation teachers tell you: Pick a time of day, preferably morning, and practice every day.

This is good advice if you can make it work, and I follow it for the most part. I can't make morning meditation work because I have kids, so my usual time to sit is at night after they go to bed. On a good day, I sit for the full thirty minutes, but sometimes I do fifteen or twenty based on my schedule or if I am falling asleep. On crazy days, I may snag five minutes in the car (while it is parked, of course) between meetings.

But what about those crazy days when you literally have zero time for anything, let alone meditation? Even on those days, you can incorporate micro mindfulness into your day.

Here are some things you'll want to try:

- *Mini walking meditation.* Simply feel your feet on the floor when you walk around the office. It may help you avoid rushing unconsciously when you have a hectic schedule or brief due by close of business.

- *The body sweep technique.* This is a mini body scan. Quickly feel the sensations in your brow, eyes, jaw, neck, shoulders, heart, belly, hips, and hands. Why those areas? Those are the places where most people tend to feel emotion and hold unconscious tension. By sweeping through, you can check in and quickly relax to help yourself feel more at ease.

- *Real deep breaths.* If you get agitated by, let's say, a nasty email or frustrating news, or yet another argument from your doting child, a few deep breaths can be a lifesaver. Now that you know breath practice, you know there's a difference between a deep breath that just forces out air and maybe some energy and a mindful deep breath which can calm and center you. In tough situations, take a few or several deep breaths to calm down so you can handle the situation better.

- *Loving-kindness in action.* You may not think loving-kindness practice is as portable as breath practice or a body scan, but not so. You can offer the phrases silently to yourself when you have to watch someone else struggling, such as when you are in a deposition with a sympathetic witness.

- *Common humanity.* If you sense judgment coming on for someone else, consider how that person is "just like me." Instead of judging opposing counsel

as arrogant or unreasonable, you can remember
that they are human "just like me" or trying to
represent their client "just like me." You can do this
for yourself to avoid judging yourself on those rare
occasions when you screw up. Instead of beating
yourself up, ask how you would treat your best
friend in the same situation.

These practices are wonderful because they are effective,
and they keep the habits of mindfulness and compassion
robust and vibrant no matter how hectic your life and law
practice get.

Given our lives as lawyers, it's possible, if not likely, that
you may start a meditation practice that helps you enor-
mously, but you can't do it every day. If you use any of the
mini strategies I just mentioned, though, you still included
mindfulness in your life, and even better, you actually used
it to directly benefit your life.

There's nothing wrong or inferior about this at all. This
isn't a lapsed habit. It's you crafting the habit breath by breath.

That's all meditation practice is. Noticing the breath or
other focal point. Drifting away. Coming back and being
kind to yourself when you do.

In this way, the question I want you to ask at the end
of this book isn't "Now what?" The question I want you to
ask, over and over again for the rest of your life, is, "What
now?" What is there for you now? And now? And now? What
thoughts are in your mind? What do you feel in your body?
What is there in your heart?

Inevitably, the frequency, regularity, and amount that
you can ask these questions for yourself will change over the
course of your life. To ensure that the benefits of mindfulness

and compassion stay in your life, however, all you have to do is keep asking them.

- What Do You Think?

Be honest now. Are you disappointed that I didn't share the secret strategy for finding the time to meditate? That's because I don't think there is one. As I've shared here, my secret was seeing how much the practice helped me and also seeing what happened when I stopped. After four weeks of practice, take the time to reflect on what impact mindfulness and compassion have had in your life. Consider what has motivated you to find the time to read this book and devote the time to practice these last few weeks.

- Next Steps

Set a long-term goal for your practice and consider why the goal matters to your life. Write it down somewhere that you can review it or tell someone else about your goal. Remember to keep your goal specific, attainable, and objectively measurable.

In addition, to keep mindfulness and compassion on your mind as you move forward, subscribe to the blog at www.brilliantlegalmind.com.

What are your thoughts or insights?

CHAPTER 10

YOU'LL FEEL LIKE A BADASS LAWYER WHEN MINDFULNESS AND COMPASSION BECOME AUTOMATIC

Here we are at the end. Now, it's time for my big closing argument before you go back to the jury room of life to determine if what you read in the previous chapters makes sense. Of course, I hope you realize that the test is not whether you have a perfect meditation practice or any meditation practice six months from now. The test will be whether you can use the practices and insights offered in this book and whether they improved your life or law practice.

In the first chapter, I promised that the practices you would learn could do just that. In fact, I said that cultivating mindfulness and compassion could make you a badass lawyer or at least help you connect with your true nature as a badass lawyer. To that end, you learned practices intended to help you develop mindfulness to settle the mind and body awareness to build comfort with bodily sensations and emotions.

You also learned joy and loving-kindness practices to help you reconnect with positive emotions and cultivate compassion for yourself and others. Finally, you discovered strategies to help you live mindfulness and compassion in your law practice for yourself, others, and the firms or organizations of which you are a part.

With all these practices, though, I hope you understand that the aim was never to change or fix you.

The aim was to help you uncover the goodness inherent in you and let it out even when the world and our law practices make that hard. Now, it may be true that you still don't know what I mean when I tell you that you are essentially good.

Perhaps you doubt this due to patterns of mind, spiritual or cultural ideas you got growing up, or because you've seen yourself do too many things you now regret. I used to be the same way, but all these meditation teachers I learned from kept talking about essential or basic goodness. Though I wasn't convinced, I got curious about it.

What I want to inspire you to do after reading this book is for you to get curious about your own goodness. How does it show up? What does it feel like? How can you know it's there?

I did this by looking for my goodness when I sat in meditation and when I was living my life. I had little more of an inkling about it until I finally saw it come out automatically during one of the most difficult moments in my life. I told you in the first chapter about the challenges I faced during my first pregnancy due to a lack of self-compassion. During my second pregnancy, about four years later and several years into my meditation practice, I felt firsthand what a difference mindfulness and compassion could make.

That pregnancy was a normal one, or so I thought, and my water broke at around thirty-eight weeks with no problems anticipated for the delivery. Despite my water breaking, though, I was put on Pitocin to speed up the dilation process because it was still a few weeks early. I had no problems with this for more than twenty-four hours until I started pushing. As soon as that happened, my daughter's blood pressure dropped, and the medical staff couldn't figure out why.

They awkwardly moved my epidural-paralyzed body around the bed to see if position might affect her heart rate but to no avail. The doctor scanned the machines, saw no improvement, and quickly ordered an emergency C-section. I didn't know what was going on, but I recall the staff saying something about a knot in the umbilical cord. Implicitly, I knew that my daughter could be suffocated if we didn't act quickly.

I had no time to prepare, I was totally sleep deprived, and the only information I had was what I could glean from the worried faces of the medical staff around me. As I lay on the bed being wheeled to the operating room, without my husband or any other supporters, this voice came to me out of nowhere that said, "The only thing you can do for her now is to stay calm."

So—amazingly—that's what I did. Tears rolled down my cheeks, but I kept my body still. I didn't mentally check out or panic internally. I am not sure how this happened, given how tired and scared I was. My only explanations are that I was able to do it because I was staying calm for my daughter and because I had practiced this in meditation hundreds of times.

My daughter is six now, but I remember every detail of that experience. Despite the activity in the room and the meds forced hastily into my IV to manage pain during the surgery, I was clear and calm enough to observe everything happening to me. Though I was terrified at the moment, I am so proud to look back now, even though I couldn't do anything. I'm proud because I stayed present for myself and my daughter when it mattered.

That presence turned what could have been a traumatic experience into one I never want to forget because I felt love pouring out of me at a time when I was terrified and totally helpless. Though I had always doubted myself and had even doubted myself as a mother, in that moment when I was pushed to my limits and all my control was taken away, goodness came out.

What I am saying, then, is that life experiences will help you get a better idea of what you are looking for in terms of your essential goodness.

With time and experience, you will likely see your goodness is there and can come out even when you don't intentionally try. The goodness I am talking about is the ability to feel what is there, receive it with kindness, and have the courage to stay present for it. Your body knows what feels good, and your mind is always looking for a reward, the good in every situation. You've learned to cut through the various things that can get in the way of clear awareness and pay attention to what's going on in your body and heart. Now you just have to practice and let that goodness come out automatically.

This is why you train to cultivate mindfulness and compassion. Lawyers are great at thinking, planning, and controlling conditions to maximize the situation for our clients. But life has a way of putting us into situations where our ability to think, plan, and control may be limited or taken away. When you can still respond with kindness and awareness, life isn't so hard.

It has happened to me in my law practice so many times. Mindfulness and compassion have helped me stay steady and trust myself when litigating difficult cases. They have helped me respond with concern when I needed to help a terrified witness prepare to testify at trial. They have helped me calm down an associate who worried about being able to manage the work of litigation and the stress of law practice. They have helped me begin to teach other lawyers loving-kindness, even though I knew that, at first, they might view it with skepticism.

If there is one thing that I hope you learn from this book, it is that this goodness is in you too.

Maybe it won't feel like the example I just described because I hope your law practice never becomes as scary as that situation. But I believe you will have times when you notice your goodness coming out without you trying. It may start small. Maybe you'll notice the person in the grocery store who needs help grabbing an item. Then you'll check in with someone in your office who has been looking a bit down. And then you'll find yourself genuinely moved when the opposing counsel you've never liked asks for an extension of time because his mother passed away.

I told you in the first chapter of the book that these practices can make you a badass lawyer. Perhaps you are thinking that these examples seem too small to claim that title. That may be because, as a lawyer, you have the power to help people in big ways. I also encourage you, though, to remember the power of helping others in small ways too.

Small things can grow and, in the right circumstances, can mean everything. When you pay better attention to what is there for you in life and develop more awareness of how things feel, you put yourself in a position to face the big challenges that scare you and do the necessary small things to cause yourself and others less pain.

Remember, I didn't write this book just to get you to meditate; I wrote it to help you see that you can change the world for the better.

I wrote this book because I believe that if enough people understood what mindfulness and compassion are and had the skill to use them in life and law practice, the world would be a vastly different place. Imagine what the world might look like if we all slowed down just a little bit. Imagine what it might be like if we all explored and understood our emotions. Imagine what it might be like if we all practiced cultivating kindness in ourselves and sending it out to the world.

I don't put the pressure on you as an individual to make huge changes across the world, but I do believe even though we have never met and may never speak that you are intrinsically good, and you have the capacity to let that goodness out and change the world. You are a badass lawyer because you are a human one. Stay connected to your humanity and go use it to serve yourself, your clients, and your community well.

• Next Steps

We have arrived at the end of the book, but that does not mean it is the end of available support for your practice. As I said at the outset, meditation is a practice best done in community. To stay connected with other lawyers and professionals who practice mindfulness and compassion in their lives and work, subscribe to the blog at www.brilliantlegalmind.com.

What are your thoughts or insights?

ACKNOWLEDGMENTS

My first thanks go to my daughters, Sophie and Elinor, who brought wisdom, light, joy, and lots of hugs into my life. To my husband, Brian, who laughs at me on occasion for all this mindfulness stuff but encourages me too and has never complained when I asked for time to meditate, attend a retreat, or write. I thank my grandpa Bob and parents, who are the first badass lawyers I learned from and taught me to be my own person but serve others in the process. Thanks to my sister, Audrey, and my uncle, Steve Hoffman, who always remind me that I am a badass even when I feel silly or weird for trying new things.

I thank my old firm, Adams Law, PLLC, for never discouraging me from writing, speaking, or pursuing training in mindfulness, and I thank my new firm, Wood + Lamping LLP for encouraging me and giving me time to write this book.

I thank my coach, friend, and mentor, Angie Taylor, for listening to me rave about how much meditation helped me and telling me I should teach it. Thanks also to so many legal and professional groups that gave me opportunities to speak early on, including the Northern Kentucky Chamber of Commerce Women's Initiative, Kentucky Defense Counsel, Inc., MothersEsquire, and so many more. Thank you to every firm, company, and organization that invited me to offer talks and training to their employees and to every audience member who told me my sessions meant something to them.

I thank every meditation, compassion, and writing teacher I have ever learned from and every friend, connection, or stranger from the internet who ever read one of my articles or LinkedIn posts or followed my blog. I thank the community of creative lawyers and professionals, mindfulness teachers, and coaches I have cultivated over the years, including Michelle Browning Coughlin and the individuals who offered testimonials for this book. So many of you have supported my work, shared ideas, or inspired me with your brilliance.

Finally, I thank my thinking mind that has driven me crazy for most of my life, but when I finally learned to regard it with kindness and curiosity, it eventually pushed me to start writing.